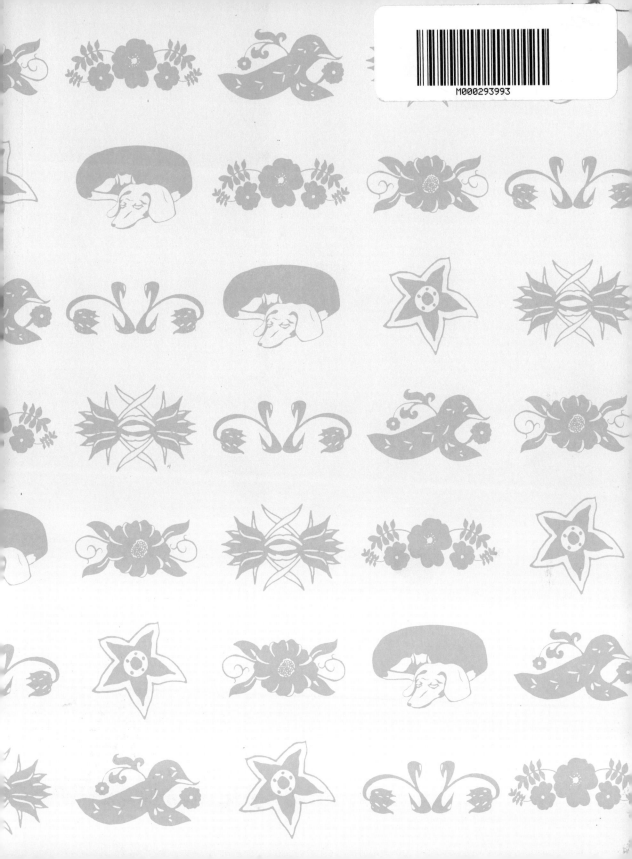

DEAR
CHRISTO

To Lyn and Jim - Staying with you in Bethaven
is always such a delight. Wish I lived
nearer. Much love,
Rosemary 24/10/11

DEAR CHRISTO

Memories of Christopher Lloyd at Great Dixter

Foreword by Beth Chatto

Preface by Fergus Garrett and Rosemary Alexander

With contributions by
Anna Pavord,
Alan Titchmarsh,
Dan Pearson
and Helen Dillon

Timber Press
Portland • London

The publishers would like to thank all those who generously donated written
contributions and photographs to the Great Dixter House and Gardens for
inclusion in the book. Picture acknowledgements appear on page 208.
Every effort has been made to trace copyright holders and any
omissions or mistakes will be corrected in future editions.

Published in 2010 by Timber Press, Inc.

The Haseltine Building
133 S.W. Second Avenue, Suite 450
Portland, Oregon 97204-3527
www.timberpress.com

2 The Quadrant
135 Salusbury Road
London NW6 6RJ
www.timberpress.co.uk

ISBN 978-1-60469-223-5

Designed by James Nunn
Second printing 2011
Printed in China

A catalogue record for this book is available from the British Library.

CONTENTS

FOREWORD

What a brilliant idea it was to bring together all these dear familiar names, so many of us – who met and enjoyed one another's company (made possible by Christo's untold generosity) – who enlivened and warmed the old house with lasting friendships, all to Christo's delight and satisfaction. Regardless of the many fine obituaries, worldwide articles in newspapers and magazines this book will warm his spirit like no other. We became his extended family and will remain so. To be able to read each other's thoughts, memories, anecdotes and share them with others will keep the spirit of Dixter alive. It will remain a bond between us. Christo would not have wished for better.

Among personal memories I treasure, one occurred during a bitter winter, when water froze on the windowsill of the north-facing kitchen at Dixter. Taking me up the wide, wooden staircase Christo collected logs from a narrow cupboard on the landing to make a fire in my room. Later as I lay hugging blankets to my chin, I watched fire light flickering over the dark, shadowy room and wondered about the generations before who had slept under Dixter's roofs.

Perhaps my funniest memory was sitting in the first class captain's lounge waiting for Christo to join me at the airport, where we were to travel to Australia, the beginning of a world tour of lectures. Other assembled guests included a group of elegant women draped in flowing white robes and expensive jewellery. Christo arrived, bustling in, clutching his ancient overnight bag. The cracked black leather peeling like fish scales. From it he extracted a brown paper parcel and offered me sandwiches, his own homemade bread and sweet ham. Nothing went to waste at Dixter! It was the beginning of a unique adventure.

Beth Chatto
January 2010

Map of Great Dixter

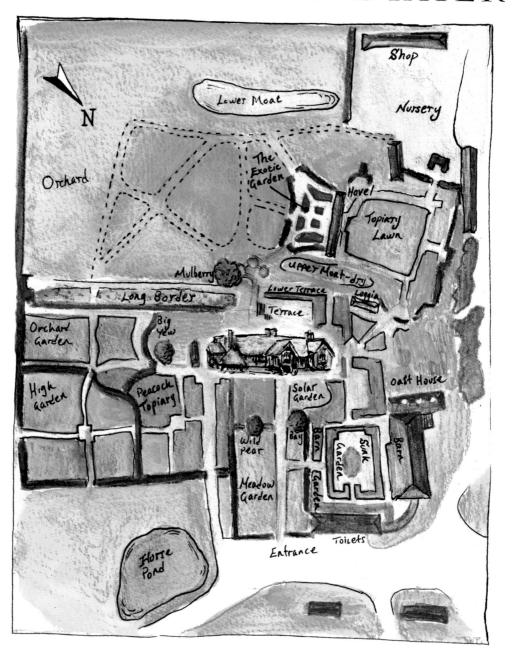

N

Shop

Nursery

Lower Moat

Orchard

The Exotic Garden

Hovel

Topiary Lawn

Upper Moat-dry

Mulberry

Lower Terrace

Loggia

Long Border

Terrace

Orchard Garden

Big Yew

Solar Garden

Oast House

High Garden

Peacock Topiary

Wild Pear

Bay

Barn Garden

Sunk Garden

Barn

Meadow Garden

Horse Pond

Entrance

Toilets

PREFACE

It is often said that Christopher Lloyd collected people, and after his death many of us in his 'collection' recalled the happy occasions and fruitful friendships we all enjoyed at Great Dixter as a way of coming to terms with our loss. As so many of us had such amazing memories of plant advice, practical jokes, delicious dinners, snatches of conversation including his famous (feared) 'put downs' we decided, at one of our regular Dixter Development Committee meetings, to gather them together in a book.

Only Christo could have drawn together so many people with such a range of interests and accomplishments. In the pages that follow musicians, artists, writers, botanists and gardeners come together to remember what Dixter means to them. For some, Great Dixter confirmed their decision to take up a career in horticulture while for others it changed the course of their lives. Visits to Dixter were memorable for Christo's cooking and the book includes his favourite recipes. His generosity in organizing opera visits, his travels and his skill as a journalist and letter writer are described, interspersed with photographs that capture the atmosphere of this very special place.

Great Dixter was, and continues to be, rather like some vast extended family, with everyone drawn together by mutual interests and a love for the place. Many of today's great gardeners who worked or spent time at Dixter describe how the lessons they learned there continue to influence their work today. The regular staff and volunteers who run the house and garden who are also very much part of the family have also provided valuable insights for the book. Linda Jones who ran the RHS Trials at Wisley for many years and is now part of Christo's extended family, working in the Dixter office, put huge efforts into tracking down contributors and coordinating the book and it owes much to her care and tenacity.

Christo loved conversation, and many evenings were spent in the solar with him and various other friends, eating olives and drinking Champagne or whisky, with the two dachshunds curled up (thankfully) in a blanket, before a most delicious dinner. Although he is no longer able to be part of these evenings his legacy continues. Thank you to everyone who has contributed to this book and to friends, visitors, staff, and students who help to keep the Dixter magic alive.

Rosemary Alexander
April 2010

This book is centred around one incredible man and his way of life. Christopher Lloyd was born and lived most of his life at Great Dixter. He was an extraordinary character, a kind, generous, intelligent man who loved people but at the same time didn't suffer fools gladly. His garden has remained a place of pilgrimage for adventurous gardeners throughout the world and his spirit and style lives on here and in his writing. He was undoubtedly one of the greatest garden writers and gardeners of all time and his influence is immense. His words in print remain his legacy and his influence burns bright in all of us he breathed life into. He changed our lives and long may his memory last.

Fergus Garrett
June 2010

ARRIVALS

I always approached Dixter through the lanes from Bodiam.
This way, there was plenty of time for anticipation to build.
From the woods, you emerge into Northiam and take the
final left-hand turn into the lane that leads directly past
the horse pond to the house and its surrounding phalanx
of outbuildings. Opening the wicket gate was almost the
best moment of all, the porch standing wonkily ahead, the
garden familiar, yet always surprising.   ANNA PAVORD

Seeing Dixter for the first time was still clear in my mind some two years later. I was collected from the London train at Northiam on a grey November morning and as I was driven down Dixter Lane, the house seemed to rise up out of the ground as if growing in front of me. It's a memory that never ceases to stir me.

BRENT MCKENZIE

Most mornings, Christopher would come out of the front door and walk up the path to meet me, always with a pleasant good morning, and ask how I was. Then we would spend a few minutes talking about our health, the weather and the garden in all its splendour, which of course was especially close to his heart.   MICK AUSTIN

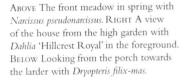

ABOVE The front meadow in spring with *Narcissus pseudonarcissus.* RIGHT A view of the house from the high garden with *Dahlia* 'Hillcrest Royal' in the foreground. BELOW Looking from the porch towards the larder with *Dryopteris filix-mas.*

Arrival at Dixter is very special as the walk down the path to the front door allows time to absorb the atmosphere of the garden and the house and the guest is greeted by the lovely, ever changing potted plant display. The experience conjures a feeling of joyful expectation of the weekend ahead, with the twentieth century left firmly in the car park.   BOB & BRIDGET WADEY

I knew that I had chanced upon what has always felt to me to be a remarkable and spiritual space. The area resonates with beauty and peace in any season. The first time I walked through the gates and saw the house, I felt like I was returning home.   MARLA ANGERMEIER

Many of my overnight visits to Dixter were in November, after the main gardening season was over. Invariably, the journey from Peterborough to Northiam was undertaken after sunset and usually accompanied by torrential rain and gusting wind. Arriving at Dixter in pitch darkness and being lashed by horizontal rain is a little unnerving, particularly as there was usually no light from the house, save for the small lit window of Christo's study. After gingerly picking my way down the path to the great oak door, I wielded the iron knocker. The sound reverberated through the great hall and then all was silent. Eventually I heard the sound of slippered footsteps getting ever louder. The iron latch clunked in its mountings and the door creaked open. "Hello, you must be exhausted. Do come in," said a quiet voice. "I'm just cooking quails' eggs, I do hope you like them. Most people do." I had arrived at sanctuary.

"What music do you like?" Christo enquired suddenly, without looking up from preparing the globe artichokes he had picked for lunch another day. "Early twentieth-century European and Russian music, particularly the symphonies of Shostakovich, Prokofiev and the works of Bartok," I answered, somewhat hesitantly. "I don't like any of those eastern Europeans or Russians, far too loud and brash. I much prefer Mozart, particularly *The Magic Flute*. Far more lyrical and light-hearted." My response was halted by a sudden loud knock on the kitchen door. "Oh, I hope you don't mind me asking someone else over, I forgot to mention it," said Christo. Before I could reply, he had barked, "Come in!" The door swung open and in stepped Beth Chatto, complete with a wooden trug festooned with fresh flowers, herbs and greens. "I picked these from my garden fresh this morning," she said breezily. "I thought they might come in useful." I was slightly taken aback that Christo had somehow failed to tell me that Beth Chatto was coming to lunch and that I was now in the company of two of the country's leading gardeners. "I was just asking Ian what music he liked," continued Christo. "I also like jazz, par-

Ian Hodgson is editor of the RHS magazine *The Garden.*

Early morning frost sharpens the outline of the *Aster lateriflorus* 'Horizontalis' hedges.

ticularly big band music," I gabbled, vainly trying to find common ground. "My father was a drummer in a big band that played Glenn Miller." "Who's Glenn Miller?" enquired Christo, "And what on earth did he do?" For a second or two there was silence. "Now Christo – I can't believe that you don't know who Glenn Miller is," said Beth, politely but firmly. "You lived through the war, surely you must have heard of Glenn Miller. He was on the radio all the time." "I can happily say I've never heard of him," he retorted. "Jazz has just never been my thing. Now Mozart, there was a real composer." It was to my great relief the conversation soon turned back to gardening.

I always looked forward to after-dinner conversations in Christo's study. The crackling log fire, a glass of brandy and verbal meanderings along the highways and by-ways of gardening. The last time we met was in November 2005 and Christo, ever the host, settled us both down in his world-worn armchairs. Unexpectedly, he suddenly produced a little notepad and pencil. "I hope you don't mind," he said, "These days I can't always remember everything I get told. So if you say something interesting I'll just jot it down on my pad for later." We started talking, about plants, gardens, people and places. Two hours sped by. Christo suddenly looked up and said, "I'm feeling tired, I need to go to bed. Thanks for your company and conversation." I looked at his pad. There was not one mark on it.

As editor of *The Garden* I had thoroughly enjoyed commissioning Christopher over a number of years and suggesting new ideas to him, to which he was usually very receptive. He always fed back his thoughts. One theme moved him more than others. "That last feature." "Yes, Christo?" I said, somewhat hesitantly, not knowing what was coming. "I liked writing it as it made me think. Liked the title. 'Plants that die with dignity.' Lovely. Just the way I'd like to go."

Christo found Wye College to be a great source of new friends over the years. We found ourselves seated next to one another at a dinner in his honour held there one night when he was invited to speak. He slurped his soup, listened to me wittering on and looked immensely bored with the company (I now realize I should have felt honoured he didn't fall asleep completely) but a week later, a plain postcard arrived in my pigeonhole inviting me to come to Dixter. For me, it was an Alice in Wonderland moment – a door in the skirting board that offered escape from normality (student pub crawls and endless card games) to something big and beautiful. Even when I later worked at Sissinghurst, I always relished the drive over to something altogether more exciting and free. Everything at Dixter is larger than life – the foliage, floorboards, flagstones, chimneys erupting from Lutyens' sensual roofs, the guests, Christo and even the plant names like *Polystichum setiferum* 'Pulcherrimum Bevis'. It's a grand fern and its name has the small distinction of being the first bit of Latin I learnt with enthusiasm.

Neil Ross is a garden writer, designer and consultant based in Somerset.

If you arrived at Dixter late, it was a bit of a job to get in. Negotiating the gate and front meadow was hard enough with only a dim sixty-watt bulb under the porch to guide you and the spooky silhouette of the house making the hairs on the back of your neck stand up. One night everyone had gone upstairs for drinks and the bell wasn't working. It took me half an hour throwing stones at windows just to get inside. I dare say it would be impossible in the dark these days, as the pots that welcome you at the door have swelled from a collection into a crowd.

It was Russian roulette who your companions would be at a Dixter weekend and there was always a sinking of heart if it turned out to be some starchy London accountant rather than a basket weaver or a relaxed American, but the surroundings were always compensation as of course was Christo himself – alternately orchestrating, growling or falling asleep. My first visit was deepest winter with the great fire in the solar, Champagne in antique flutes with glass as thick as the bottom of a beer bottle and the scamper of the dachshunds heading for their blanket, a sound which still reminds me of leaves blowing down one of the York stone paths.

It was a bit of a gamble which room you were given to sleep in and there was a definite pecking order. I began my career there in the night nursery, the high ceiling leaning drunkenly against the back of a great chimney stack with beds you could drive a train under. Once you had climbed in, the crisp leaden sheets and the sag in the middle made it impossible to get out again – especially with a hangover in the morning. The room had one continuous bookshelf wrapped around three walls. Most worryingly, the bookshelves sagged like the beds and the books were an inch deep in dust so I rarely slept well, as I was wondering if the whole lot might collapse on me in the night. The plumbing

Views of the house from the exotic garden where the planting includes *Ricinus communis, Colocasia esculenta, Musa basjoo* and *Pennisetum setaceum* 'Rubrum' (left) and from the horse pond at sunset (above).

was also vaguely threatening and had a life of its own. The water for the great footed baths always came out the colour of tea and the plugs were so ill-fitting that on one occasion I remember preparing for a luxuriously deep plunge only to nudge one with my foot as I leapt in. So generous was the bore of the pipe that after a frantic tussle with it, five seconds later I found myself beached in the empty bath, having used up all the hot water that particular afternoon.

I was eventually promoted from the night nursery to a dainty bedroom beyond the yeoman's hall. It had a frilly four poster bed and dressing table with mirrors so fogged up with age that you looked positively Dickensian in them. One wall of the room was nicotine brown with the plaster ruptured like a sheet of scrumpled newspaper. I found that very satisfying but it's been restored now. On many nights I pored over gardening books till the small hours with the ticking of the clock and the creaking of the house, which on windy nights sounded like it had ambitions to be a galleon on the high seas. This dark, cosy room was a cave from which one emerged into the brightness of the garden in the morning. With luck, one's day in the garden would be preceded by one of those Enid Blyton breakfasts Christo did so well: thick-cut marmalade, a bowl of stewed apple, cream – the works.

The best bedroom had a log fire and was reserved for the chosen few – most often Beth Chatto. Beth is only little so it seemed a bit of a waste; you could have fitted a football team in there! Beth was a great companion to have at Dixter – she was as authoritative and opinionated as Christo but she brought a motherly kindness and warmth. Beth would always be helping out with the cooking and would stick up for you in a dinner time debate. Dinners were always a highlight. We would tuck into far too many drinks in the solar or yeoman's hall first. In summer, the door of the latter would be left open. A single fat *Magnolia grandiflora* bloom would often be found squatting on a polished table, revealing its lemon-meringue scent, or it might be a single

piece of *Cestrum parqui* picked to perfume the whole room as small bats flitted in and out, somersaulting high in the rafters.

Everyone had a job to do – at lunch it might be to descend to the basement to retrieve Champagne or beers from a ridiculously inconvenient cellar tucked into the billiard room. On the way down, chicory was often found sprouting in big terracotta pots in the gloom and you might be asked to pick that, or to bring in some violets and primroses from the garden to put into a salad. More trusted guests got out the best silver from a huge safe or did the cooking. I, for my part, was trusted with nibbles – cashews and shriveled up olives which I grew to love.

So many things today take you instantly back to Dixter days – the smell of an old church, a crumbly slab of good cheddar and a hundred iconic plants. By chance tonight I'm sitting with the first flower on my newly acquired *Cestrum parqui* and the smell is carrying me back to Dixter as I sit here. Like his dogs, Christo had a lovable side but he could bite too. He was never quick to praise people and could be very short with them, but in me he sensed a spark of enthusiasm all those years ago and was generous enough to take the trouble of beckoning me through the door. Dixter is inside me now – a bright flicker that spurs me on – and for that I will always be grateful.

A bloom of *Magnolia* 'Galaxy' (above), *Cestrum parqui* (left) and a nasturtium-dressed salad (right).

My first view of Dixter from the front gate, on a summer evening nearly sixty years ago, is one of my strongest and fondest memories. Christo and I were colleagues at Wye, and I had been invited to Dixter for the weekend. The grass on each side of the path was, I think, well mown, but my eyes concentrated on that beautiful house and the big front door through which I was welcomed by Mrs Lloyd.

My room in the top of the house was known as the cook's room, though there had been no resident cook for some years. After enjoying the view across to Bodiam Castle, I found my way to the solar where I found Christo with his brothers, Quentin and Pat (who was home on leave) and sister, Letitia. Her husband, Nils, was working in Lebanon. A very young Olivia (daughter of Nils and Letitia) had been put to bed.

I began to learn how Dixter worked. Christo's mother, Daisy Lloyd, known within the family as The Management, came to say goodnight to us all at about seven o'clock and then we discussed what was available for supper and who should complete the preparations. After the first of many meals that I was to eat at the table in the servants' hall, we washed some glasses, cutlery and coffee cups in the pantry and left the rest in the kitchen for the day staff.

On Saturday I saw the garden and found – or was given – plenty to do but only remember picking peaches for supper from the big tree trained against the east wall of the house. On Sunday afternoon I was invited to Mrs Lloyd's sanctum, the yeoman's hall, and we had a good long talk.

That was the first of many visits. By 1957, the house and gardens were open daily and I stayed for some weeks acting as house guide. Tips went into the Restoration Fund and were used to buy gin. Dixter was never a place for idleness. On one occasion I became too engrossed in scraping algae off the wall of the pond in the sunk garden and was late for lunch. This was The Management's meal of the day and I was in the doghouse for the only time I was ever aware

Bob Seeley is a retired agricultural biochemist.

BELOW *Camassia quamash* in the front meadow garden. OPPOSITE ABOVE Narcissus bulbs ready for planting. OPPOSITE BELOW *Tulipa* 'Prinses Irene' underplanted with forget-me-nots.

of. My jobs were mostly deadheading or weeding, but I remember one Saturday morning when Christo and I planted the lime tree at the west end of the lower moat.

I have been unable to visit Dixter since Christo died but it is good to know that under the leadership of Fergus, its special atmosphere remains.

Gerry Dawson works as a freelance cameraman for the BBC.

From the moment that I first saw Dixter in early morning spring light I was beguiled and also thrilled to think I would be able to observe and record its beauty for a whole year.

We were filming for the BBC television series Gardeners' World and often started work between seven and nine o'clock in the morning. At that time of the day, we had the garden largely to ourselves. The gardeners were of course already hard at work, but if we needed a free space they would oblige. Many of my favourite shots were made during these peaceful early hours of daylight.

It didn't seem to matter what the weather was doing or what time of year it was, at the start of each day I was always sure we would find any number of wonderful images. As we spent more time at Dixter I came to really appreciate how it changed with the light. Very early it became clear that our film had not two but three major characters, Great Dixter, Christopher and Fergus.

I clearly remember the first time we heard the novel way that Christopher would call for Fergus, with a couple of short blasts on his air-horn out of the study window. I know that we wanted to include it in our programme but I have a sneaking suspicion that Christopher vetoed it!

I can also recall the morning that Christopher turned up with a kitchen timer set for twenty minutes. He said that it was to remind him that he had some artichoke soup on the stove for lunch. At least an hour later we, but not Christopher, realised that the timer had not been working. Nothing more was ever said about the soup.

Christopher's pieces were never scripted because we wanted to try and capture his thoughts in a natural way. We were often more than happy with his first take especially if it had some Christo sparkle – an indefinable twinkle in the eye and some wonderful words.

GARDENS & GARDENING

But what we remember most is waking early and peering out the mullioned bedroom windows at the garden below – it was like awakening in a wonderland. The tentacles of the settled fog wound through the garden. It was so enticing that we threw on our day clothes, grabbed our cameras, and crept through the silent house into the garden. We had it to ourselves, alone in the shrouded, quiet garden where the sense of history and design was enchanting and mesmerizing.

NANCY GOLDMAN AND LUCY HARDIMAN

Most of all, we remember something Christopher said one day that has inspired us ever since: "A garden should be thick with incident."
IAN HOOPER

RIGHT Looping string round the stem of a dahlia prior to staking. BELOW LEFT TO RIGHT: using a clove hitch on tarred twine to stake a rose to a cane; taking a dahlia cutting; watering a tray of succulents. OPPOSITE TOP TO BOTTOM Fergus Garrett working in the long border; plant sales at the potting shed; lifting cacti and succulents for overwintering.

I soon discovered that Dixter was so much more than a garden. Dixter was, and is, a way of life.
C. COLSTON BURRELL

Christo always said that in designing a personal garden you should try to make only one person happy – yourself.
Jeff Jabco

In the sixties, my father gave my wife an annual subscription to *Country Life* for her birthday. We had no significant garden then, but Christo's witty articles caught my fancy, so when I visited Dixter, I nosed him out in that lovely potting shed tipping out a six-inch pot of rooted clematis cuttings. He captured my imagination and interest with his enthusiasm for propagation and the plants he produced.
Patrick Bates

When we decided to update our own gardens through the creation of a large mixed border, our objective was to adapt to our climate and soil the principles of succession planting and colour blending that are so elegantly demonstrated at Dixter.
Eliot Wadsworth

Sneaking alone into the exotic garden to become lost in its Rousseauesque fantasy. SID JONES

The impetus for change or "replant disease" as Lloyd calls it, provided the catalyst for the exotic garden. It is a late summer to autumn garden with a tropical effect. Many of the best foliage plants are quite hardy. Cannas and dahlias provide the major colour display with assistance from *Verbena bonariensis*. Foliage plants like *Musa basjoo* and *Arundo donax* dominate visually, while *Ailanthus altissima* and *Rhus glabra* 'Laciniata' respond well to being cut back and *Eucalyptus gunnii* and *Phormium cookianum* 'Tricolor' provide striking contrast. SCOTT SCARFONE

ABOVE Looking from the hovel into the exotic garden. OPPOSITE Vibrant colour in the exotic garden with *Dahlia* 'Witteman's Superba' and *Verbena bonariensis* in the foreground.

Peter Knox-Shaw gardens with his wife Barbara outside Cape Town, South Africa. He is also the author of *Jane Austen and the Enlightenment*.

One byway of horticulture that Christo explored with characteristic gusto was the management of garden visitors, and over the years he honed a number of replies to irksome stock questions that he was happy to impart. If asked how many people work in your garden, he would say, be sure that you answer, "Never enough – would you like to volunteer?" And his advice to gardeners faced with the inquiry, "And when is your garden at its best?" was, "Always say 'now.'"

Any gardener who follows Christo on this point will be saved from the pitfall of explaining (according to temperament) either how much better things recently looked, or how wonderful they soon will, but at the risk of perjury for most. On Christo's lips the words had truth, and even took on special meaning. "It is through our strong sense of mortality," he wrote while reflecting on the fragile radiance of oriental poppies, "that ephemeral beauty is so keenly savoured." An acute sense of transience in the plant realm underscored his whole approach to gardening. Not for him the single mental snapshot to which all efforts should be geared, but rather a creation that answered to all times, that unfolded like a musical composition, continuously developing its themes, and raising surge upon surge of sensation, if not bloom, through each season. Plans for sustained effect were laid in his first book, *The Mixed Border*, which offers many 'plots' for sequential planting, and such contrapuntal wizardry was taken further in *The Well-Tempered Garden*. But in his later work, both in and out of doors, Christo increasingly added to this classical strain a romantic yen for the flamboyant and exotic. Overlooking both topiary and meadow, the gardens of Dixter bridge that greatest of stylistic divides as securely as the music of Brahms. At once spontaneous and strategic, they couple taut form with voluptuous expressiveness, while uniting different worlds.

Seldom well-tempered when it comes to season, nature did Christo proud when he visited the Cape at the end of August in 1999 in search of promising plants. Along the west coast he gazed to his heart's content at daisies, some new to him among many old favourites. On another trip he was enchanted by the tiny garnet heads of the wax creeper *Microloma sagittatum* clinging to fire-blackened stems above a sea of *Moraea villosa*. He was soon in love with a long list of plants that included the rabbit-eared *Anemone tenuifolia*, the dark-eyed *Drosera cistiflora*, the deep red form of *Babiana stricta*, and the astonishing blue variant of *Sparaxis grandiflora* that rises like a Bristol goblet from the pink soil of the Tulbagh valley. Though the odds were greatly against him, Christo was ready to give anything a go, short of transporting a burnt field back to Kent. This zest for experiment is still very active at Dixter today, giving it the advantage over other old gardens that have been preserved to the letter at the expense of their original spirit. It is for this reason that there can only be one answer to the question, when is Dixter at its best? Now.

ABOVE *Magnolia × soulangeana* 'Lennei' and *Magnolia stellata* in the distance. BELOW *Tulipa* 'Queen of Sheba' in the high garden.

John Emmanuel is the Assistant Director of Horticulture at Wave Hill garden in New York, U.S.A.

Mecca of gardens, Great Dixter remains the ultimate destination for me. Its wonders have fired my imagination for years. Great Dixter is not the unapproachable haven of a dreamer but the very real work of Christopher Lloyd, a singular gardener, an artist, and a great writer. He meticulously offered up the lessons of his lifetime of gardening at Great Dixter. It was through his books I became familiar with the garden and the man.

It's hard to imagine any other garden writer who has written as many books, all based on one garden. *The Mixed Border* was written when I was eight. Most of his other books were written before I had even dreamed of living a gardener's life. I hadn't even heard of Great Dixter until I took up professional work at Wave Hill where, of course, it was well known to my own mentors, Marco Polo Stufano and John Nally. When I first perceived its glow through Lloyd's own words in *The Well-Tempered Garden*, I was working at another garden that, like Great Dixter, was ahead of its time. Since its publication in 1973, *The Well-Tempered Garden* remains enveloped in a luster of authenticity that lies on it like a patina on ancient ruins.

I saw Great Dixter refracted through Lloyd's descriptions, which also describe every aspect of gardening imaginable. When he explained that *Magnolia × soulangeana* 'Lennei' is "a large sprawling shrub rather than a small tree" wasn't this one of the oldest inhabitants of the garden, growing near the terrace wall? When he wrote, "If you are burrowing into and among plants in a border, you should do as much as you can from one position because the more often you move, the more havoc is your frame likely to wreak," wasn't that the great man on all fours, yanking out errant chickweed near the red *Tulipa* 'Dyanito' in the long border?

He was already slightly stoop-shouldered and had that familiar crop of white wavy hair when I actually met him in the mid eighties at Wave Hill. With John Nally, our curator of collections, he surveyed our new flower garden. To John's

delight he said, "Something interesting is going on here," and began asking a lot of questions. Up at the aquatic garden, Lloyd asked John why we had planted three Ravenna grasses in a small circular lawn bed when one would suffice. Unfortunately, every writer is at the mercy of his readers. In *The Well-Tempered Garden* he had written that one ornamental grass would seem "self-conscious" all alone, three would be better. But Lloyd never wholly subscribed to any one gardening formula. He saw what the physicality of our site required and Marco agreed, so the other two grasses were removed.

Lloyd visited Wave Hill twice more in the nineties, bringing with him his right-hand man Fergus Garrett, who is now in charge of Great Dixter. Christo's gait had slowed and he took naps frequently, but his enthusiasm seemed stronger. In our eyes Christopher Lloyd had always been a man unafraid of using the wildest colours in the wildest combinations. His reputation was partially built on his use of colour. He was a celebrity in the garden world, yet it seemed to him a bit of a joke. And that's why we loved him. Christopher Lloyd was not just a great author and renowned gardener, he was one of us.

ABOVE *Cyprus papyrus* with *Dahlia* 'Chimborazo'. OPPOSITE Unidentified tulip which came into the garden as 'Burgundy' but has yet to be accurately identified.

Tom Wright has spent a lifetime working in professional horticulture. He has lectured at Wye College and internationally, sat on the National Trust Gardens Panel for over twenty years and wrote and contributed to many horticultural books during his career. He currently works as a garden and landscape consultant.

My memories of Great Dixter are closely bound up with those I have of Christopher Lloyd himself. I first met Christo when he was a lecturer and I was a student at Wye College, now some sixty years ago.

As a keen plantsman and inspired lecturer, Christo used numerous living plant specimens collected from the College gardens and from Dixter to illustrate his lectures, which proved to be popular and inspirational. Christo soon detected those of us in our group who were especially keen on plants. A chosen few of us were then invited to stay at Dixter for short weekends. I was lucky enough to be one of these, and after Saturday morning lectures and seminars we would leave for Dixter in Christo's car with strict instructions from his mother not to be late. Lunch at Dixter was always served promptly at half-past twelve.

My initial sight of Dixter was an unforgettable and magical experience. The first glimpse of the old half-

timbered house and its reclining porch, partly hidden by well-clipped hedges and specimen trees, gave me a hint of what we were to see. More was revealed as we approached the house through the now famous meadow garden along a wide York stone path. We learned later that many of these bold flagstones were salvaged from London pavements during the building of the garden earlier in the century.

After lunch, Christo's mother, Daisy, led us round the garden. She wore flowing skirts, held a trowel in her hand and was also carrying her favourite trug basket. The intricacies and surprises of the garden layout were quite overwhelming. The many structural features of the clipped hedges, topiary groups and specimens, stone paths and finely constructed steps to enclosed gardens were matched by many different plant associations and planting schemes. It took me many visits to really understand and appreciate the garden at Dixter.

On Sunday mornings we would tour the garden again – there was no church-going custom at Dixter – before returning to Wye after lunch. These visits gave me an insight into the important part Daisy played in Christo's upbringing and in developing his knowledge of and love for plants and gardens. Christo's father died when Christo was only eight, leaving his mother the huge responsibility of bringing up a family of six children, as well as developing the gardens at Dixter. It is, therefore, not surprising that she came to be known at Dixter as The Management. She proved to be a passionate, energetic and successful gardener.

I returned to Wye as a lecturer in 1968, and was very proud to be able to follow in Christo's footsteps. Garden studies and visits became an essential part of the syllabus and trips to Dixter became a regular fixture in my courses, as I had kept in touch with Christo and he was very willing to receive student groups. By then, he was becoming famous as a garden writer and the garden was also changing under this control.

He could be intolerant with those who only had a passing interest in the feast of plants at Dixter. I recall a student in one of my groups casually asking him the name of a rather special aster. Christo gave him the name and became quite irritated when the student failed to produce a notebook to record it. Among one of the students within these groups was Fergus Garrett who was later to become head gardener at Great Dixter.

David Culp is owner of Brandywine Cottage, a nursery in Pennsylvania U.S.A. that specializes in hellebores.

One cannot help but feel the creative force at work at Great Dixter. It saturates the garden like the colours Christopher Lloyd used and permeates the pages written about it. I fell under Dixter's spell long before my initial visit.

I remember a sense of reverence as I walked down the path to the garden only to later learn that reverence was a word of which Christopher would seldom approve. One noticeable exception was perhaps in relation to the procedures of gardening. This was made even more evident the first time Christopher visited my garden. Feelings of honour were interspersed with panic as Christopher, Jeff Jabco, and Joe Henderson arrived for a visit and lunch. What could I offer a man from whom I had learned so much? He put me at ease right away by taking out his notebook and asking questions about my plants and taking notes. (I had learned before that Christopher expected people to take notes!) The Master himself was one of us. Pausing to take pictures, to take notes, and to ask questions, the man who knew a great deal about gardening never stopped learning. His love of learning, his unstoppable passion for plants and his quest for knowledge are things that I admired and loved in the man.

During the visit, we discussed the merits of certain plants and colour theories – with the freedom of not having to always agree. It was far more important with Christopher to have an informed opinion. Our discussions often took place in the garden, but also around the table surrounded by good

FROM THE TOP A sport of *Dahlia* 'Stevie Dee' which occurred at Dixter, *Meconopsis cambrica*, *Dahlia 'Dovegrove'*, and *Dahlia* 'Magenta Star' with *Eucalyptus gunnii*.

friends, good drinks, and good food. It was all about the complete experience.

Christopher loved to cook as well as to garden. Suffering from a great void in my own culinary skills, I wondered just how Christopher seemed to do it all. One day, as we were walking around Dixter, an alarm started going off in Christopher's sweater pocket. He smiled and pulled out two alarms with the explanation that they were set to go off when certain items needed attention in the kitchen – another epiphany of a different sort.

His great love of all aspects of his garden, his willingness to share and most importantly, to always learn, are things I will always cherish about Christopher. He held a special light for me on the garden path and he continues to do so. Thank you, Christopher Lloyd.

Orchis mascula growing in the meadow.

Chris Baines writes frequently in BBC *Gardeners' World*, BBC *Wildlife* and *Country Living* magazines.

Crinkle-leaved parsley was the plant that first captivated me at Great Dixter. I visited in the revolutionary year of 1968 and was surprised to find anarchy afoot even in horticulture. I was then a student at Wye College and all the students and I felt that we had a special link with Christopher Lloyd since he had been teaching there only a dozen years earlier. Nevertheless, I had no idea what to expect. I recall the great man showing us the famous long border, accompanied by two particularly snappy dachshunds – I also vividly remember the parsley. It was planted as carpet bedding, tightly packed beneath colourful annuals and I remember it seemed both out of place and perfect at the same time. With hindsight, it should have been no surprise. There are few plants that can match it for colour and texture, and clearly it could never have been confined to the vegetable patch in the garden of such a free-thinking plantsman.

Choosing to champion garden wildlife has always put me in no-man's land between purist horticulturalists on the one hand and single-minded natural historians on the other. Back in the sixties and seventies, wildlife in a garden was only ever seen as a pest, a weed or a disease, whilst nature conservation was restricted to native plants and animals in remote reserves, maintained exclusively for a privileged few. The meadows at Great Dixter occupied a

Erythronium dens-canis.

very reassuring middle ground. The green-winged orchids, fritillaries and cowslips in the orchard were recognisable replicas of those in the meadows found in more orthodox nature reserves. This showed that such domesticated landscapes could offer a refuge for the wildflowers that were rapidly disappearing from the farming countryside.

By comparison I found the flowery meads to either side of the path to the front door even more inspiring. At a time when the lawn mower manufacturers were still promoting perfectly striped lawns and the natural history zealots were still pursuing the purist preservation of native species, Christopher Lloyd was paying no attention to either. His rough-cut grass was sprinkled with a whole variety of flowering plants. Some of them were native, but many were not. Bulbs and corms from the eastern Mediterranean, herbaceous perennials from South Africa and North America, primroses, anemones and cowslips from the Sussex countryside – together they formed a tapestry of colour that was worthy of a medieval wall hanging. Fifteen years after that first visit as a student, Christo's flowery meadow spurred me on to introduce my very first wildlife garden to the Chelsea Flower Show.

BELOW CLOCKWISE FROM TOP
A mown path dissects the meadow; *Camassia quamash* in the front meadow; *Camassia leichtlini.* OPPOSITE *Fritillaria meleagris* in the orchard.

It was the dynamic nature of Christopher Lloyd's garden that made it so unique, while his endless willingness to pass on his enthusiasm made the man so important in his lifetime. The garden itself remains in the best of hands and will certainly evolve, but the true Lloyd legacy will be the way Great Dixter continues to capture the imagination and broaden the outlook of budding gardeners in the decades to come.

I first met Christo in the summer of 1995. A complete novice, and a gardener only in my imagination, I was hoping to embark on a horticultural career at the age of twenty. Fergus showed me into the great house, where the old man was sitting in the dining room over his raspberries. "What's your experience?" he asked sharply. In reply, I mumbled evasively about pulling out weeds in my mother's garden. Looking up sternly from under his brow, he cut me short: "You'll have to watch him, Fergus." So ended the interview, and so began my life as a gardener.

I was given a month to prove myself and I tried very hard. I remember becoming frustrated at having to spend long afternoons shelling peas; my precious time there was slipping away! I loved the garden and was curious about everything in it; I carried a notebook wherever I went. For myself, there is no better place I could have been – not just to begin learning my trade, but also for inspiration. I owe more to that month than probably any other in my life.

Nowhere could have fired my youthful imagination like Dixter did, nowhere could have affirmed my new choice of career so thrillingly. Christo's apparently advancing age seemed a front – his mind stayed keener and younger than most young minds are. He knew every plant in the garden down to individual vegetables, but if that sounds prosaic I should point out that the plantings he created with Fergus were nothing of the kind. Everything here

Rory Dusoir worked as a gardener at Great Dixter from 2000 to 2003.

OPPOSITE *Anemone* x *hybrida* 'Honorine Jobert'.

was zesty, original, exhilarating, and deftly executed. His planting ideas often seemed to provide an affront to fusty establishment figures and to prevailing fashion all at once. In a conservative world, he was a natural provocateur because he was always himself.

Christo loved youth, and I suppose that made him all the more conscious of growing old. He enjoyed passing on the benefit of his experience to young and enquiring minds. He once sat down and explained his predilection for Japanese anemones to me, and for *Anemone* × *hybrida* 'Honorine Jobert' in particular, because it is long flowering but always fresh and elegant to the last, with no need to dead-head. We were at the eastern end of the long border, which at that moment, he told me, was his favourite part of the garden. I could not but become a gardener after that July. I was incredibly lucky to have spent the first few weeks of my new career in the presence of a master at the peak of his powers. How many others did Dixter touch in this way? I used to take advantage of my lunch-break to take notes in the garden. Once Christo appeared with a guest. Anxious that I risked being late back to work, I asked them how close it was to two o'clock. His guest replied, "Twenty to; you have plenty of time." The old man suddenly looked distant. "Yes, he has plenty of time," he said.

Simon Folkard was a gardener at Great Dixter from 1978 to 1991.

It was always a slight source of irritation to Christo that the process of clipping the yew hedges always lasted from September until well into the next year. There were two main reasons for this during the ten years that I was responsible for them. Firstly, I was working only three days a week at Dixter at the time and secondly, Christo always said that I had to get a billiard table finish when clipping those trees.

One occasion is indelibly cast in my memory. Christo would invariably take a stroll at about ten o'clock in the morning to collect ideas for his writing. On one such November morning, I was clipping the inside of the rose garden, as it was then. The swirling wind was blowing a penetrating gale as I wrestled to fight down my billowing ground sheets among the unforgiving and unpruned roses. As Christo passed, he remarked on the abundance of haws in the nearby thorn tree before going on down to the nursery. I knew he would reappear as usual at four o'clock, after his post lunch nap, and I also knew that I had a battle ahead to achieve, as I saw it, an acceptable amount of progress before his return.

Despite my battle with the sheets, I soon discovered that most of my clippings were hurtling away and coming to rest in the by now despised roses! It had been emphatically instilled upon me by my predecessor, Albert Croft, that when tackling this marathon task on no account should any clippings be left uncollected for the boss to find.

Well, it doesn't take too much imagination to appreciate my apprehension as four o'clock approached. I knew my progress had been wanting but all in all I rationalised that with the conditions as they were, I had done as well as could be expected.

On the dot of four o'clock, preceded by Sweetie Pie and Crocus, the man reappeared and commented, "You haven't moved from where you were this morning!"

My worst fears had materialised. The predictability of the situation only fuelled my frustration. Then to cap it all, the dogs decided to set about tearing my ankles to shreds. This unprovoked attack went ahead without the least bit of concern on the part of their master.

To be fair, there was absolutely no malice in Christo's observation, even if it was a tad insensitive. However, due to the preceding period of anxiety, and predicting such an outcome, I bit back. It was, to be honest, more a nip than a full-blown bite. I mumbled some inanities about the elements and the stupid roses hindering my normally unopposed progress. Despite the disgruntled undertone by

which I made it known that he had not fully appreciated my problems or efforts, to his credit my comment was met with one of his disarmingly enigmatic smiles. He compounded my exasperation by saying, "Well, I expect you'll achieve twice as much tomorrow!" after which he strolled off, seemingly oblivious to the culmination of an awful day at Great Dixter.

I knew very little about plants but I had other skills that stood me in good stead at Dixter. After graduating in Fine Art from Maidstone College in 1986 with no enthusiasm for poverty, I subsequently trained as a carpenter and joiner, which is how I have supplemented my career as a painter over the years. I cut the Dixter hedges over about forty days in the winter of 1992 – the razor edge became an obsession and this has parallels with how I draw now. The way I go about constructing and resolving pictures compositionally now has definitely been informed by my experience of working at Dixter.

Christo was hugely frustrating because he was so tickled by the contrary and controversial view. Ironically, I think he was conventional in many ways but radical in approaching conventions in a provocative, almost cavalier fashion. As I recall, he was an agnostic verging on the atheist and I remember a small incident when I was installing the new garden bench overlooking the topiary garden around 1992 or 1993. I was fretting about some invisible detail on the underside of the bench I had made and I quipped to him that it didn't matter because no one could see it. He replied, as one agnostic to another, that God could see it. The childish maverick in him was an inspiration. God bless you, Christo.

Jonathan Lloyd is an artist who lives and works in Northumberland. He worked at Great Dixter for a period during the 1990s and made a number of gates and benches for the garden.

Dan Pearson is a garden designer, author and weekly gardening columnist for *The Observer*.

I caught the gardening bug early, at the age of five or six. By the time I had read *The Well-Tempered Garden* in my early teens, it would be fair to say I was obsessed. Christopher's words made perfect sense to me as I pored over the paragraphs. Every June, my father and I would take a trip from Hampshire to visit Sissinghurst and Dixter. I can still remember the excitement at seeing Dixter in the flesh and feeling that the sense of freedom in gardening I had felt when reading *The Well-Tempered Garden* was right there in the gardens before me. I loved the fact that the garden felt so lived in and was imperfect but real.

Our gardening practices were a little on the wild side at home and our orchard was one of the most magical places in our scruffy acre. A border backed onto the orchard and I soon became fascinated by the idea of using grass in my gardening. My father suggested I write to Christopher to ask if he would show me his meadows. To my surprise, he wrote back with an invitation to come and a date was set. On the day of my visit, we spent at least a couple of hours walking through the garden. I remember feeling distinctly that I was in the presence of a great gardener, but he did not present the garden in a way that was remotely intimidating. To a new gardener, a beautiful garden can be frustratingly full of mystery, but Christopher presented an experiment, not a finished product. He made it clear that his gardens were a work in progress and that without experimentation, one was never going to learn. As an adult, I can now fully appreciate what a generous gift his advice was, considering all the demands that were made on his time. I came away with my head buzzing and a belief that I had found my vocation in life.

Jonathan Lloyd's work including a pencil drawing of the low meadow (opposite far left), a detail of the exotic garden bench (opposite left) and a detail of his Lutyens gate (above).

Christmas 2003. I was new to the garden world, as I had just become part of a photographic collective in Brixton known for its soft, neutral tones and people portraits. I should have seen the signs, but at the age of thirty-one I began working with intensely coloured plant portraits, developing ways to exploit colour in the printing processes. At the time I had a very old, small Nissan car so Kent and East Sussex were about my geographical limit. I was aware of Christo's and Fergus' work with colour (partly through Jonathan Buckley's photographs) and so I set my sights on Dixter.

Heartened by the welcome I received from Perry when I called the office, it was soon February 2004 and I was on a white-knuckle ride to Dixter at four o'clock in the morning. I was greeted by a perfect sunrise with a cover of snow – what an incredible place, even in winter without the beds in flower. I felt an overwhelming excitement, a quickening and although it was my first visit, I saw the flow of the light around the property straight away so I began taking some photographs very quickly. A little too quickly as it turned out: after an hour or so I somehow dropped my camera on the flagstones by the long border. The back broke off and

Allan Pollok-Morris is a photographer who regularly photographed Great Dixter between 2004 and 2006.

smashed while the roll of film was ruined and the camera unusable.

I had a spare in the car, but the snow was melting and the light and moment had passed. I felt disappointed, but also lucky to have some rolls shot and safe. It was early morning so I messed about photographing in the harsh white light for a while. I felt a little better about it all when the biscuits I brought went down well during the morning tea break. It was such a pleasure to meet Christo, Fergus and Perry for the first time.

For me, Dixter remains a very positive reminder of the chance moments people experience when starting out in new ventures. It is often a rollercoaster of trial, error, risk, reward, discovery and disaster. Looking back, my first arrival at Dixter was typical of the warm reception with which the garden world nurtures "new bees", generously giving us lucky breaks like the one I feel I had at Dixter that morning.

Two years later, the photos I took at Dixter that day were published as a magazine feature with Christo's words. It was a real privilege to have such a legendary writer put his words to my photographs.

Photographs taken by Allan Pollok-Morris at Great Dixter between 2004 and 2006.

Gardening baffles me. I can do houses but not gardens. Houses are obedient dogs, waiting patiently to know their master's bidding. Gardens are feline, nature and nurture in constant argument. Leave them alone for a minute and they will strive after some state of nature. They are second cousins to chaos. As Kipling reminded us, Adam was a gardener. Original sin began with an act of pruning.

My first acquaintance with this subject was to sub-edit Lloyd's weekly column in *Country Life*. He sensed at once that I could not tell a poppy from a peony. He was an irascible perfectionist, and we had constant trouble with illustrations. These were still in black and white, and when delivered from the library were, as far I could see, identical. The art department simply touched up the same print each week to look like what was allegedly depicted. This understandably infuriated Lloyd. When I suggested that our editing was no less iconoclastic than his gardening, our relationship abruptly ended.

Yet Lloyd could be a kind and generous man. He had the appearance of a retired colonel and welcomed thousands to Great Dixter. Women of a certain age doted on his bachelor naughtiness, sublimated into doing something dreadful with lobelias. This was perhaps his response to an overbearing mother, nicknamed The Management. Young students from Wye College braved his dachshunds and enjoyed his steak and kidney pie. Anyone who was serious, very serious, about plants would be admitted into the great conversation that is an English garden.

One of my most satisfying jobs in the garden at Great Dixter was harvesting the vegetables for Christopher Lloyd and his many guests. Occasionally, he would ask me what was ready to eat but I think this was a test. He knew exactly when each vegetable would

Simon Jenkins became Chairman of the National Trust after working as a journalist and author for many years. This extract is taken from a column published in *The Guardian* on 3rd February 2006 shortly after Christopher Lloyd's death.

OPPOSITE FROM THE TOP
Favourite vegetable garden tools, work in progress, and freshly dug pink fir apples.

Perry Rodriguez has worked as a gardener at Great Dixter for many years in a variety of roles. He is currently Business Manager at the garden.

be ready for the kitchen. He knew this from his years of experience and because he loved everything he chose to grow in his garden. He monitored and enjoyed its progress through all its seasons.

As a gardener, the tools of my trade are very important to me. You soon develop a preference for particular tools and learn that different models of forks and spades can make a big difference to the job at hand. I am very fond of sharp, shiny and well-worn spades.

For the job of vegetable harvesting a sharp knife, and sometimes a garden fork, would usually suffice. But you also need a container to collect the produce in and to take it to the kitchen. Over the years I had always enjoyed using a size eight Sussex Trug, made from willow and chestnut wood. But when I began working at Dixter I noticed that Christo had a few baskets that were different shapes and sizes for this task. They were not traditional English gardening baskets, but they were robust and very attractive. They had all been brought back from Turkey as gifts by the head gardener Fergus Garrett who is half Turkish.

When you have raised a crop from seed, nurtured and protected it from every predator under the sun (including the dachshunds) harvesting the produce is a very significant moment. I would choose which baskets to use according to what vegetables Christo wanted to cook. Strong for Pink Fir apple potatoes, the round lightweight one for raspberries, and the longer one for leeks and celeriac. When all the vegetables were scrubbed and trimmed I would arrange them in the baskets and leave them on the teak draining board. However, my pride was dented occasionally when Christo informed me with relish that if he asked for fifty sprouts he did not mean forty-nine.

These last two years Fergus and I have travelled to Turkey, with one highlight being a visit to the basket maker in Istanbul. We sat in his workshop and watched him at work. His craftsmanship was exemplary. He ordered us tea which we drank while he worked. I bought a tall chestnut kufe, a basket used for carrying loaves of bread, which I am very proud of and hope he overcharged me for.

My day would start at quarter past eight in the dining room, opening the post with Christo. This would include plant orders for the nursery. Over a cup of Lapsang Souchong, we would decide what was available and in autumn and spring I would assemble the plants. In April, this would involve walking up through the old orchard and meadow to lift the necessary plants. In autumn, I would invariably pass an old Blenheim apple tree and would eat an apple every time I passed it.

Winter could be a difficult time. On cold, bright days a large number of heavy glass lids had to be lifted off the cold frames and stacked at the end of the rows. They then had to be replaced later in the day if frost threatened. If it threatened to be a very cold night, a roll of hessian would also be applied to act as extra protection for the young plants inside – effective but labour-intensive.

One of my winter jobs was to weed and mulch all the young trees in the meadow using compost made from stacks of hay cut in the late summer. The older heaps of rotting

Tom Shephard was head gardener at Great Dixter for nearly eight years.

Fergus Garrett cutting the meadow grass.

hay were planted with ornamental gourds which were later also sold in the house. The compost heaps were a haven for grass snakes and they often made their nests there. We once surprised one of the snakes in the dining room. It had come in through the open garden door and was drinking the cat's saucer of milk. It gave an irritated "Hiss!" and slithered out again.

Christo had a very large collection of clay pots into which fast growing plants like cistus were potted for sale. They had to be watered two or three times a day in hot weather and there was always a pile of pots to be cleaned in winter. Pot washing gave some respite to freezing hands when no other work was practically possible, the clay soil being frozen solid. It was done with scrubbing brushes in an old copper pot under which a fire was lit early in the morning. Soil sterilisation was another warm but unpleasantly dirty job, involving a huge dragon's breath of flame blasting through the soil. A further winter task was to delve down into the gloom of the cellar once a week to water the chicory and sea kale that Christo grew there to produce pale and delicious shoots for the kitchen. Then one might visit Christo for consultation or orders in the parlour where he would be sitting in front of a huge blazing hornbeam fire writing with his two beloved dachshunds Crocus and Tulipa warmly snuggled in their basket and pieces of his exquisite tapestry lying on a chair waiting to be completed.

I can honestly say I learned practically everything I know about plants and gardening from working with Christo at Great Dixter and was able to use his ideas in my own garden in Scotland to good effect. Christo visited my new garden there twice and he and Beth Chatto were both very enthusiastic about my efforts to garden in the face of the North Atlantic.

It is a truth universally acknowledged that a television producer in possession of a good gardening series must be in want of Christopher Lloyd. In this case, the logic was inescapable as *Over the Garden Wall* sought to explore the habitats of familiar garden plants and their wild relatives. Where better to see this botanical transaction than at Great Dixter? The location was still better given that the focus of the episode was meadows and grasslands.

The plan was to start filming at Great Dixter and then venture out onto the white cliffs of Dover. As May 1993 came to an end, the meadows running up the front path at Great Dixter were awash with colour, with bold oxeye daisies (*Leucanthemum vulgare*) and common spotted orchids (*Dactylorhiza fuchsii*) peeping through. By the horse pond lay the wet meadow complete with still more common spotted orchids. Christopher resolutely resisted mentioning just how the orchids got there but their arrival was certainly decades before the 1981 Wildlife & Countryside Act arrived to bring protection to wild orchids! It was certainly amazing that in 1993, less than fifteen years after the Act, native

Dr Anne-Maria Brennan was the producer of a BBC TV series of which an episode was filmed at Great Dixter.

orchids had become so popular among gardeners that there was a ready supply of perfectly legal, artificially propagated plants.

Passing through the then young prairie garden, we entered the orchard with its ocean-like meadow. Patting an apple tree I made my first faux pas, referring to the tree as "an old veteran," to which he added, "I planted that one myself." Oops! Oh how I worried about the careless line, only to later discover just how patient, kind and learned the great gardener was. It was at that moment that Christopher Lloyd became Christo to me. I even passed what might have been a bizarre initiation ceremony, stroking Dahlia throughout an interview, only to discover (once the camera had fallen silent) that she had taken a chunk out of the local postman less than a week before!

Cut to the white cliffs of Dover and the tortuous cliff paths that thread their way across the downs. The talk was of cabbages (or rather their wild relatives) and kings. A comment was made that Roman emperors used viper's bugloss (*Echium vulgare*) as a treatment for snakebite. The scientist in Christo came out when he exclaimed, "I wouldn't like to test that theory!" As the walking, talking and filming went on other tales were told. On seeing the wild carrot growing in its native habitat, Christo remarked that he had once eaten it along with cauliflower, potatoes and chicken and that it had "tasted of nothing," and "was quite off-putting."

Over the years Christo, Fergie, Canna and Dahlia became part of the warp and weft of my gardening life. The talking, walking, eating and drinking as well as meeting fellow famous plantsmen and women – such as Beth Chatto. There was also the reading – wise and witty words that continue to inspire me just as much as the garden itself.

OPPOSITE Evening in the orchard meadow. OVERLEAF Meadow at Great Dixter with *Dactylorhiza fuchsii* (common spotted orchid), *Leucanthemum vulgare* (ox-eye daisies) and *Lotus corniculatus* (bird's foot trefoil).

S arah: My successful supper party last night of tarragon chicken and pears in syrup inevitably reminded us all of Christopher Lloyd. Both recipes came from my well-thumbed copy of *Gardener Cook*. To me he was a very generous man, free with his time, knowledge, hospitality and inevitably, his opinions!

The first time I visited Great Dixter I was an inexperienced gardener from Kew, on a staff outing of the Decorative Department, organised by Brian Halliwell. The two of them showed me how much there is to look at, think about and disagree about in gardening. There were many subsequent, inspirational visits that were quite often enhanced by meeting Christopher. He would point out what pleased him most (and least) in his garden and also comment positively or with mild criticism – both equally useful and welcome – on what I was doing at Sissinghurst. He was always controversial, always stimulating.

My final memory is of a lunch at Great Dixter with my husband, Jim, when Christopher was becoming quite frail. The meal, delicious as usual, was followed by a walk around the garden that involved more sitting than walking. It was a reminder that one of life's greatest pleasures is to rest in a garden while musing on life and horticulture.

It is impossible to quantify what I have gained from being part of Christopher Lloyd's circle of gardening friends but I shall try: certainly greater horticultural insight and interest; plentiful inspiration from his garden; hopefully an understanding of how different gardening styles can succeed; and of course all the recipes in his book. Perhaps I can say that without him I would be a less rounded person.

Jim: Christopher came late into my life, but I had admired his books and articles in *Country Life* long before I met him. While working in Kent and East Sussex as a National Trust Gardens Advisor, I visited Great Dixter on many occasions and found the plantings both bold and innovative. I particularly remember seeing the tropical plantings (that replaced

Sarah Cook and Jim Marshall. Previously head gardener at Sissinghurst Castle Garden, Sarah now runs a successful and international garden consultancy practice with her husband, Jim Marshall.

the rose garden) in their first year and have to be honest in saying that my first thoughts were, "What a dreadful thing to do to a historic rose planting!" I was soon convinced, however, that Christopher's policy of change and innovation was right for Great Dixter, and the failing roses were replaced by a highly imaginative, luxuriant and colourful display.

Brian Halliwell is a noted British plantsman and author of numerous books on gardening.

I was at a horticultural conference in the late sixties and at lunch I was sat next to Christopher Lloyd. I did not know who he was and he did not know me. He turned to me and said, "I understand you come from Kew. Tell me, who is responsible for the appalling bedding?" I answered, "I am!" I had just taken up a new role there. In subsequent years I always invited him to Kew to inspect my summer bedding.

Christopher always gave me his honest opinion, which sometimes I did not care for. Some he liked and said so but others he didn't and pointed out why. Many of these bedding displays were afterwards written up by Christopher in *Country Life*.

One day when we were walking around Great Dixter, as we passed the topiary he said to me: "I have always wanted to get rid of these but I daren't. My father planted them and they are now part of the history of Great Dixter."

Kathleen: In November 1985, I saw an advert in the local paper advertising for two gardeners to work at Great Dixter. I hesitated, not knowing if I had enough experience to apply for a job at this world-renowned garden. I'd already had five years' experience working on two nurseries after leaving Hadlow College and was unemployed at the time, so I thought I had nothing to lose and plenty to gain. Christo himself phoned me to arrange a date and time to come along.

The interview took place in the parlour by the roaring log fire and was very informal. Christo sat opposite me, while Quentin, his brother, sat to one side. Christo asked me a few basic questions, such as, "Can you water plants properly?"

I'll never forget the moment when I proffered my CV and references over to Christo and he immediately peered over the top of his glasses and said in a gruff voice, "I don't bother with those bits of paper." Finally, I asked him if I would be taking my instructions from the head gardener and he said in a commanding voice, "I'm the head gardener!"

Kathleen and Philip Leighton. Philip Leighton is a landscape gardener. He is married to Kathleen Leighton, Nursery Manager at Great Dixter.

Philip: Over the years, I have had the privilege to call Christo a friend, as that was the way he always treated me. He was always a very generous man, as we found out when we lost our first dog, a Sussex spaniel called Jake. When Kathleen told him about it, he said, "When you get another I will pay for it," which he did. It is something we will always remember as Ginny, our springer, was the best dog anyone could wish for and lived to the great age of seventeen.

Kemal and Nicola Mehdi.
Kemal and Nicola Mehdi lived
next door to Great Dixter
between 1982 and 2004.

Kemal: Our extended family moved next door to Christopher at the end of 1982. We lived in the cottage by Dixter's fruit cages. I had first been taken to Dixter by Tom Wright when I was studying at Wye College and had been a frequent visitor ever since. Christopher was an excellent neighbour and we quickly became good friends.

On one occasion in midsummer 1984, we were in the yeoman's hall talking about garden conservation and evolution. Christopher was very clear on the subject of Dixter. The garden should reflect the tastes and ideas of its owner and/or head gardener. He was pleased to the point of being smug that there were no comprehensive or detailed plans of the Dixter plantings. "No future head gardener can ever be told to use the plans and restore the garden to exactly how Lloyd had it in 1984," were his exact words. Christopher was referring mainly to relatively short-term plantings rather than the longer-term structures of hedges, trees and larger shrubs. He certainly did not want the future Dixter gardeners to be fettered by the past. In his view, allowing the future gardeners to have fun with consistent but gradual experiment and change would allow the garden to develop in an evolutionary way.

One winter evening, we were over at Dixter for supper when Christopher showed me a picture in a book of a shallow lake in Malawi with crinums piercing the surface across a vast expanse of water. The idea intrigued Christopher and a few days later I came across Rick, one of the gardeners, digging in the shallows of the horse pond. Not the best of jobs for a winter morning, as it must have been cold in the water, but crinums were to be planted and preparations must be made. I kept an eye on the spot and the crinums duly appeared, but never really got going and the clump died out.

Some years later I was surprised to notice a crinum flowering at the edge of the horse pond. I assumed that somehow the clump had managed to survive. When I mentioned it to Christopher he was immensely pleased (with himself), "Oh, you don't think I gave up? No, I had it replanted and on the second attempt it established."

Nicola: While pottering around in the kitchen soon after moving in, I noticed Kemal hovering near one of the entrances into the Dixter vegetable garden. At the time, the garden was shaded by a walnut tree planted by Christo's mother. Kemal was almost hopping with excitement and I realized that something was definitely going on. Before I could ask what was about to happen, Christo sidled up the path with a downward gaze, with a pair of dachshunds hanging back and looking on warily. Genial greetings were exchanged and the dogs were shushed as the questions began.

"An interesting name. Oh! A working gardener, where did you learn to garden?" asked Christo. Kemal replied, "Wye, with Tom Wright." Christo smiled. I slipped closer, sensing that these two obsessive gardeners were likely to wander off in a haze of Latin plant names and disappear to Dixter without me! "You must come to dinner!" exclaimed Christo enthusiastically, and then with a slightly offhanded tilt of his head and in solemn, quiet tone he added, "Oh, and you can come too." I felt this was a challenge and that a quick response was needed or he'd be gone. I looked him straight in the eye and said, "It hadn't occurred to me that I wouldn't come too." Kemal's shoulders tensed, and then a huge guffaw came from Christo and was followed by, "Very good, very good. Eight o'clock on Saturday then!"

For just over twenty years our lives were loosely entwined, as the views from our rear windows showed us Dixter. When we moved just two hundred yards away it felt like arriving in another world, such was the power of Great Dixter to transport you into a different place. I sensed at Dixter a timeless quality, one which radiated from the red bricks and tiles of the house and was enlivened by the play of light across the southern aspect of a Sussex ridge.

Cornelia Steffen lives (and gardens) near Great Dixter.

Dear Christopher,

After the last visitors had left, I slipped into the garden today and sat on an Edwin Lutyens bench to admire the exuberant display of the long border, seemingly unaffected by this summer's drought. I noticed that there was a tiny little bit of the house to be seen – something you did not want to see from this position, if I remember correctly? Would you have argued with Fergus about the trimming of the hedge, I wonder? Would you have had one of your mutual discussions you once referred to as much loved duels with florets? If you could have seen the high garden this summer, I am sure, you would have been overwhelmed. In almost fourteen years of visiting Great Dixter, I can't remember seeing this part of the garden so overflowing, so excessively lavish.

Thank you for every one of your visits to our garden. They put me into a frenzy to get every plant to the utmost perfection. I luxuriated in the positive comments but also remember fearing your awkward little smile accompanying your finger, pointing to something you definitely disapproved of: "What is thaaat?" No, dear Christopher, you were not for the faint-hearted, surely not. Fortunately for me, you loved my cooking, the conversations with my husband Hartmut about classical music and his Bach performances on his cello (you were the first person for whom he overcame his natural shyness – thank you).

I could not sit very long on your favourite bench today. Two little barking monsters came running towards me. Canna, so feared in the past, took my whole hand into her mouth to give a welcome-chew and then, even Yucca started whimpering - and off we went together for their favourite walk, through the meadows, down to the woodland and back through the garden into the house.

View through the orchard to the long border.

A love of good food, plants and a shared sense of humour was the foundation on which the friendship of five men was based. My uncle (the late John Treasure), his partner Johnie Haylock of Burford House Gardens in Worcestershire, Gordon Fenn and I would meet with Christo on many occasions to swap plants and good tales. We Treasures of the group also shared a distant relation with Christo – Oliver Cromwell.

I recall one magnificent evening when Christo and Fergus were staying at Burford House, which is famed for John's collection of clematis. After enjoying a sumptuous and rather grand dinner we took the candelabras off the table and proceeded into the garden where we placed them around a pool. The scene was magical and we continued to partake of wine and chat until well after midnight. Christo would love to stir up discussion so our conversations were always very stimulating.

When not together communication between us continued in the form of letters. Christo was a prolific letter writer and often corresponded with long letters that would take us days to decipher (he would have made a good doctor!)

Raymond Treasure & Gordon Fenn are the owners of Stockbury Gardens in Herefordshire.

LEFT Allium seedheads among *Campanula patula* and poppies. OPPOSITE *Allium hollandicum* and *Tulipa* 'Blue Amiable'.

"You were where?" he asked. "Oh yes, Sissinghurst," he repeated after hearing the answer, a shaggy dog's self-conscious reaction to an overly groomed poodle. I always gravitate to the shaggy dog. Poodles are pretty, but too much maintenance.

He, of course, was Christo. Christo the colourist, Christo the texturist, Christo the fearless gardener of the incomparable Great Dixter. Christo, the man so wonderfully opinionated that he set new horticultural standards and raised the bar on garden creativity. A man who knew how to think outside the box before thinking outside the box was cool.

John Trexler is the Executive Director of the Tower Hill Botanic Garden in Massachusetts, U.S.A.

LEFT Dill with *Gaillardia* × *grandiflora* 'Burgunder' and *Scabiosa atropurpurea* 'Ace of Spades'.

THE PLANTS

Each visit to Great Dixter saw me bringing back plants to Munich or our home in Tuscany. They are still flowering: *Ceanothus* 'Puget Blue', *Daphne pontica*, and *Choisya ternata* with its scented white blossoms in April like a cloud! And you may believe me or not, but I see his white hair and white moustache among these blossoms and hear him speak to me.

FRIEDBERTH WEBER

Christo proudly showed me a clump of *Fascicularia bicolor* strapped into the guttering at the back of the kitchen and said, "It's an idea Fergus and I are trying out. Most people grow *Fascicularia* in pots or in the garden, but they are really epiphytes in the wild. All they need is an occasional soaking with fresh water. They'll certainly get this when it rains, but they won't become soggy and rotten. I think we'll see more people trying to grow them in this way in the future. A new type of pinecone perhaps." Ian Hodgson

A seat tucked into the yew hedge at the end of the long border is a great spot to rest and contemplate. As you sit on it looking down the full stretch of the border, there is an *Astelia chatamica* to the left while, *Anemone* × *hybrida* 'Honorine Jobert' dances alongside *Scabiosa atropurpurea* 'Ace of Spades' to the right. I recall Christo telling me one day how he loved to sit here and watch Canna, his beloved dachshund, as she ran towards him up the border. Cathal O'Sullivan

Giving each other plants is part and parcel of any gardening friendship. I still grow ferns that he gave me and still give me great pleasure. One of the plants I gave Christo that I know to be still thriving at Dixter is a nice form of the biennial *Campanula patula* (pictured page 60). Fergus recently put it up for an award with the RHS Herbaceous Plant Committee. JOHN FIELDING

OPPOSITE *Fascicularia bicolor* (above) and *Scabiosa atropurpurea* 'Ace of Spades' (below). A selection of dahlias grown at Great Dixter.

I met some of my favourite dahlias here – 'Hillcrest Royal', 'David Howard', 'Chimborazo', 'Yellow Hammer', 'Pearl of Heemstede', and the delicious apple potato 'Pink Fir'. CLARE LE BRUN

"Do get that *Euphorbia palustris*," said Christo one morning at an RHS Westminster show. "It's such a good plant." And on another, as I was wavering over *Ceratostigma willmottianum*, "It'll never survive with you." This was, I hopefully believed, more a reflection on our Dumfriesshire climate than on my cultivation skills. Bravely, I paid no attention and under a warm wall it gives pleasure today as I write. ALLEN PATERSON

ABOVE *Euphorbia palustris* among forget-me-nots.
RIGHT *Crocus* 'Snow Bunting'.

The scent of wintersweet will always remind me of Dixter. In winter, flowering stems would be placed in vases in the dining room and guest bedrooms infusing them with its characteristic aroma. JOHN WATKINS

We find the time to go and look at things that should be looked at. Today it was a little cluster of the tiny white *Crocus ochroleucus*, which had opened wide to late autumn sunshine. Fergus swore it was sweetly scented. That made me drop to my knees, on the damp lawn, only to discover no scent at all. Old age? Perish the thought.
From a letter to BEVERLEY McCONNELL *from* CHRISTOPHER LLOYD

When I worked at Washfield Nursery in the eighties, Christo would occasionally make an appearance at the nursery himself, often with a house guest who was staying at Great Dixter. Washfield Nursery had always been an innovative nursery, sourcing rare and new plants from British gardens and from around the world. They also bred many new plants.

On a bright late spring day, I had my first meeting with Christo at the nursery, and I remember to this day the combined sense of excitement and nervousness that his presence stirred in me. As Elizabeth Strangman's apprentice, I very much stayed in the shadows, all ears to what plant or topic was being discussed. At one point Christo's eye was drawn, predictably, to a retina-searing scarlet-flowering plant growing in a pot in the bulb frame, *Ranunculus asiaticus*. It received his closest scrutiny. Wanting to make an impression, I stepped forward and offered my observation that many ranunculus shared the common character of stained markings to their leaves. This observation did not go down well. My plant knowledge was firm enough by then, so I decided to stick to my guns by spouting a number of examples, including our own native celandine. Christo's disinterest was total and he moved on without saying a word. Clearly a marked green leaf was no match for a scarlet flower, but I had just survived my first (among many) Lloydian put downs.

Soon after this visit I received a phone call from Christo inviting me to Dixter for a walk round the garden. My acceptance was based on the confident assumption that there would be several members in the party and that it would be relatively easy, yet again, to bring up the rear. Approaching the garden on that evening after a hard day's work moved me profoundly. The tranquillity of the horse pond, the slumbering bulk of Dixter's huge tiled roofscape set against a clear early-evening sky and the fresh, tussled front meadow spangled with a kaleidoscope of spring bulbs made an impression that has never left me.

My knock on the door produced lots of barking, a gen-

Graham Gough and his wife, Lucy, established the nursery Marchants Hardy Plants in Sussex in 1998. This extract is taken from a piece published in the horticultural journal *Hortus* in Spring 2006.

eral hound commotion, a terrifying rebuke from Christo (fortunately aimed at the dogs on this occasion), the opening of the door and – alarmingly for me – Christo's solo appearance, as he said, "I have an article to write – inspire me!" It proved to be a magical, and at times testing, evening. Christo was never better than when he was on his home ground and I learned very quickly that one's arguments had to be backed up with very sound evidence. The foundation of a long and mutually affectionate friendship was in part laid in the garden at Dixter that evening.

Ursula Buchan is an award-winning garden writer. She wrote her first article for *The Garden* while studying for the diploma in horticulture at the Royal Botanic Gardens, Kew.

When I was a young trainee gardener in the mid-seventies, I used to visit Great Dixter from time to time, since a good friend of mine, Romke van de Kaa, was Head Gardener there. Many people have spoken of the interest that Christopher took in young people, especially anyone interested in horticulture, and my experience was no different. He was kind and hospitable, and extremely keen to nurture any impulse towards plantsmanship, but I remember, too, how broad his cultural interests were, and how generous he was in fostering those in young people as well.

Twice he invited me, with others, to the opera at Glyndebourne, something I could not have hoped to attend otherwise. I remember in particular a marvellously dark and atmospheric production of *Don Giovanni*. In the long supper interval, he conducted us around the garden, in particular showing us the mixed borders, about which he had been consulted. It had been a hot day and was still a warm evening. To our astonishment, he borrowed matches from a cigar-smoking opera-goer and set a clump of burning bush (*Dictamnus albus* var. *purpureus*) alight. I have never seen this done before or since. It was somehow typical of Christopher, that he should have found a very particular and unusual way of engaging our interest in plants.

We met Christo on our first visit to Dixter in the late eighties. We were in the sunk garden at the time and I had recognized the reddish-brown froth of the New Zealand burrs in fruit. "It's *Acaena novae-zelandiae*," I said to my wife. Christo was within earshot and he came over to chat, impressed by the sight of my diligent notebook and the overheard Latin.

I think he soon realised that my botanical knowledge was not as extensive as he'd guessed from hearing that beautiful name, which had remained with me from a five-year stint as an editor working on botanical encyclopaedias. But by this time I was a poetry editor and Christo also appreciated poetry, most especially heartfelt, well-crafted verse –Vernon Scannell was a favourite. And my wife, Diana, ran a literary festival at nearby Charleston, a house and garden less grand than Dixter but rich in artistic associations. So we passed the test.

Then came the first invitation to a weekend at Dixter. Once or twice a year we would drive down from London and then we'd be drinking Champagne under the waving wand flowers on the terrace with a small group that would often include writers as well as Christo's gardening colleagues.

His was a family of high standards in all things. During the war they had taken in Jewish refugees with whom he remained in touch throughout his life. Christo was defiantly original in everything he did. In his last few years he began to cook, using whenever possible ingredients from the garden – he was, of course, brilliant at it. I remember especially tasting Christo's venison with Cumberland sauce made with mustard, ginger, redcurrant jelly, port and orange peel – a delicious combination which I vowed to try myself but never did.

One August weekend in 1995 stands out. Christo revered his mother but that didn't stop him ripping out the rose garden she had planted and installing billowing cannas, banana plants and his own favourite *Verbena bonariensis* in place of the rose garden. At lunch (monkfish followed by

Peter Forbes is author of the book *Dazzled and Deceived: Mimicry and Camouflage*. **Diana Reich** is Artistic Director of the Charleston literary festivals in Sussex.

morello cherry tart), Christo told the young gardeners that they should read more poetry after which he called on me to define poetry for the assembled company. After dinner the Milky Way was clear in the sky and there were shooting stars. I don't think I'd ever seen a shooting star before that evening. How fitting that my first sight of one was at Dixter. Christo blazed his own trail – as a singular teacher and as a man who loved plants, the arts and good food. He was a whole planetary civilisation in himself, one which we satellites were happy to orbit.

After a long stint immersed in the poetry world I now find myself writing about nature. I'm sure that Christo's bold, individualistic attitude to plants was a great spur in giving me the confidence to make the switch.

Maurice & Rosemary Foster. Maurice is a plantsman who is particularly knowledgeable about woody plants. He and his wife, Rosemary, have a fine collection of trees and shrubs in their garden in Sevenoaks, Kent.

Christo maintained that it was a good idea to take cut flowers, fresh vegetables or home grown fruit as a present when visiting a friend's garden, rather than garden plants. Cut flowers would eventually be discarded, fresh produce would be consumed and enjoyed without delay, and that was the end of it. It would prevent your host possibly being put on the spot when you asked on a subsequent visit how your wonderful tree or shrub was thriving when it had not done well, was a miserable specimen, or had even died. Your host would be forced to invent lame excuses about rabbits or deer and would blame you for your generosity.

Coming to lunch with us one day (bringing plants!) and seeing the table all set in readiness in the plant-embowered small conservatory, he whispered knowingly to Rosemary, "I suppose you've been doing a spot of tidying up here before we arrived?" Lunch at Great Dixter was vastly superior and served by Christopher himself – he was a grower, producer, cook and waiter as well as a memorable host.

He had his reasons when he famously decided, much

to the discomfort and chagrin of the Royal National Rose Society, to grub his rose garden. Spraying roses fortnightly from May to October was always a chore. Inconsistency, we cried, when we discovered in the sunk garden the lovely 'Comtesse du Cayla', a fragrant aristocrat in silky coral salmon. "Ah," he said, "I couldn't possibly dig up the Comtesse as she was planted by my mother when I was a small boy and was one of her favourites. And anyway you need to have a black spot somewhere in the garden in order not to disappoint the visitors!" We talked of exotic French rose names and speculated about the inevitable exotic beauty and grace of their namesakes.

Christopher later sent us a photograph of a bust of the beautiful Comtesse du Cayla, an elegant lady, clearly distanced from the proletariat and well up to the quality of her rose namesake. Rosemary subsequently sent Christo a postcard portrait of a frowsty Madame Pierre Oger. You could tell by contrast that she had been the wife of a French nurseryman or a working lady during her life and was not quite the Comtesse's equal in the glamour stakes. Such is the romance of the rose.

I am writing this with a picture of Christo looking down on me so I hope he would approve. I first got to know him on the Royal Horticultural Society (RHS) Committee B (now the Woody Plant Committee) where his eclectic and challenging views added not only to our horticultural knowledge but also to the liveliness of our meetings.

He had an engaging way of changing his mind about plants. I remember his comments in a *Country Life* article on *Aucuba japonica* 'Picturata' of which he said, "Not a bad plant, better when stooled regularly but better still when treated with sodium chlorate." When a magnificent exhibit of *Aucuba* was put in the old hall some time later, he said, "Do you know, I really rather like it." Perhaps this was not

Lawrence Banks and his wife, Elizabeth, manage the Hergest Croft Gardens in Herefordshire.

altogether surprising since he and I shared an ambivalent attitude to variegated plants in general with a particular admiration for *Castanea sativa* 'Aureomarginata', one of the oldest cultivars recorded at Hatfield by the Tradescants, of which there is a good specimen here at Hergest Croft.

This brings me to another enthusiasm of Christo's, which was his *alma mater*, Rugby School, where I followed him some years later. We both remembered the great sweet chestnut under which we sat watching cricket as schoolboys.

In company with many others I benefited from Christo's observations, of which some were apparently obvious, but were often neglected. The one that I remember best was his comment that "Plants don't usually grow well in the dark." It made me look at my garden and realize that large areas of it were effectively sterilised by conifers of no great importance. Out came the chainsaw and lo and behold we had new places to plant. I just looked up at his photograph and I swear that he winked.

David Creese works for the Westminster City Council and has responsibility for Parks and Open Spaces in central and south London.

Rosa 'Perle D'Or' in the barn garden.

Towards the end of a summer's day in 1994 at the Victoria Embankment Gardens, I was busily sorting out a canna border when a rather sharp voice cried out, "Do you know the name of that variety of canna?" The canna was nearly as tall as me and I knew exactly what it was. "Yes, it's *Canna* 'Musifolia'." "Oh, and who laid this border out?" The voice asked. "It was me, why?" I replied somewhat anxiously. And from that day, a special relationship developed.

I was invited to his house to stay the weekend, which was a little puzzling as I had only spent about half an hour talking to him, but I was intrigued and wanted to find out more, so I went. The house was in East Sussex and was called Great Dixter. It didn't register with me at the time. I travelled to the agreed station and was met by Christo at the ticket office. We drove to his house through Northiam to Dixter. When we drove down the lane by the horse pond, I was taken by surprise as the house came into view. Once we had stopped, I couldn't get out of the car quickly enough. Christo opened the gate and as I walked down the path I was greeted by a huge building with a massive wooden entrance and a fantastic pot flower display by the porch. Christo opened the door and a very old house smell percolated outwards as I was led in. "I'll show you where your room is and then we can go out into the garden." Then the magical journey began to unfold.

Christo inspired. He may not have known it, but in his quiet way he pushed us to think harder and see more – to focus on which plants make each other look better and to critically observe plants, not just look for their flowers. Few have had his advantage of having tried to grow everything in their own garden. He was a true expert, even if the term *connoisseur* may be too old fashioned a word for someone who was always so forward thinking. Christo was always experimenting and thinking of next spring.

He was generous and expansive with his time to those of us who shared his focus – on good plants and on good food. He introduced us to broad beans and summer pudding. Christo and Fergus have frustrated us all by making wild meadows look easy. I miss him.

John Gwynne is a landscape architect who has worked extensively with the Wildlife Conservation Society. He and his partner Mikel are the owners of Sekonnet garden in Rhode Island, U.S.A.

Christopher Lloyd was a very conscientious member of the RHS' Floral Trials Committee, regularly attending the fortnightly meetings and closely scrutinising each plant on trial at Wisley. It is always good to have an outspoken member or two in a committee and Christopher Lloyd filled the bill admirably for the Floral

Linda Jones was Trials Officer at the RHS from 1992-2008 and now works at Great Dixter.

Trials. He was never at a loss to give an opinion and his succinct comments proved invaluable for the reports on the trials. He would champion certain plants that he considered should be brought to the attention of gardeners, such as *Helianthus salicifolius* for which he fought valiantly to get an award throughout the trials, but in vain.

John Massey is an expert on hellebores and hepaticas and owner of Ashwood Nurseries in the West Midlands.

My first memory of Christopher Lloyd was at an RHS show at Vincent Square. Philip Baulk and I had just completed our first ever display of the *Lewisia* species and cultivars. Christopher came to look at our stand, put his arm round me and said that he wished he could be young again, so that he too could start another genus. I don't know whether it is his encouragement, his warmth or his mischievous sparkly eyes that I miss the most.

The last time he showed me around the garden at Great Dixter he needed to take a rest at every bench. When he was ready to get back up on his feet, I would crouch a little and he would put his arms round me. As I did so, he would chuckle that he could easily get used to this. Later that day, Aaron prepared us an excellent lunch with artichokes from the garden. Christo warned us that he would probably fall asleep during the meal (and he did), but he insisted that I must not leave, because he still wanted to show me more of the garden.

Tim Miles is head gardener at Cotswold Wildlife Park & Gardens and an expert on tropical and exotic plants.

Christo's conversations were never dull – he was never one for idle chit-chat. I really identified with his sense of mischief. He so enjoyed offering up something unexpected or contrary which at the very least stimulated interesting conversation and occasionally (possibly unintentionally – though one had one's suspicions) provoked a much stronger reaction. On these occasions, while the odd individual may have been left miffed, everyone else concerned felt richer for the moment.

I clearly remember the occasion of my first stay at Dixter. On sitting down for dinner I was most disturbed to see that a large bloom of *Magnolia grandiflora* was the centrepiece of the table. "How could anyone cut such a glorious flower from its tree?" I inwardly exclaimed. However, as the evening progressed I found myself becoming involved in an increasingly in-depth study of the flower, taking into account the detail of its central floral parts, along with the wonderful colour and texture of its tepals, not to mention its delicious perfume, which is at its strongest in the evening. The more I thought about it, the more I realised that far from being a heinous horticultural crime, this had in fact been an act of inspired educational theatre, as this particular blossom was being displayed in its full glory to a highly appreciative audience.

In itself this was not a life-changing event. But my time spent with Christo was a series of such happenings, which stimulated and stretched my thinking in many ways.
Roy Lancaster once asked me if I'd ever been on a nocturnal garden walk at Dixter and I could very proudly answer that I had – with Christo! In fact, this took place on the same evening as the aforementioned dinner. Two shrubs in particular caught my attention that night, Itea ilicifolia and Cestrum parqui. Neither have particularly flamboyant floral displays and so they had never previously turned my head – but I literally saw them in a whole new light that night. Now I always associate them with Christo.

Dachshunds were always part of the fabric of Dixter and also featured in Christo's writings from time to time. On one occasion, my dog Gemma visited Dixter with me. I understand that she was one of very few other canines ever to tread into Dixter territory. She was a wonderful garden dog and caused no horticultural hassles during the weekend. Unfortunately, the then incumbents of the Dixter dachs-

A variety of artichoke called 'Gros Camus de Bretagne'.

Patrick Rice-Oxley lives in the village of Battle and is a retired doctor.

hund dynasty, Dahlia and Tulipa, did not extend the same kind of warm welcome to Gemma as their master did to his guests. Gemma tactfully avoided any confrontation for most of the weekend, but on Sunday she followed Fergus, Christo, the dachshunds and me into the confines of the sunk garden. This proved to be most unacceptable to Tulipa who broke into a passionate and sustained yap. As Gemma sidled slowly towards us the yapping became even more intense as Tulipa bravely inched backwards away from my nonplussed and largely disinterested dog, until eventually… plop! Tulipa was fully submerged in the pond and deploying a swimming style with which I was unfamiliar.

"Could this be my last visit to Dixter?" was the thought that immediately came into my mind. My momentary horror quickly dissipated as Christo was reduced to a prolonged state of all-enveloping laughter, with his cheeks turning a jolly crimson.

Not being greatly given to hero worship, I have only once in my life written a fan letter. The letter in question was to Christopher Lloyd on his seventieth birthday, thanking him for the transformative effect his writing and his garden had had on my life. I couldn't help adding a footnote to say that my *Melianthus major*, which he had assured me in one of his books was hardy once established, appeared to be dead. He replied on a postcard which I still have, thanking me for my kind words and assuring me that my melianthus was not dead but resting. Of course, he was right.

My sole encounter with the great man came as something of a surprise. I was standing on the flagged path that runs up to the front door at Dixter, gazing through the gap in the yew hedge at the barn garden and wishing I could achieve something like that at home, when he appeared at my side. He had, I suspect, popped outside for a breather after a particularly good lunch. He was extremely affable, quite unlike the curmudgeonly figure of legend, and seemed disposed to conversation. So, not wishing to pass up such an opportunity, I asked him a question about the pruning of his *Hydrangea villosa*, to which I in fact already knew the answer, having read about it in one of his books. I was afraid he would demand to see my notebook and pencil, which I understood to be his practice when asked questions by visitors, but he gave me the expected answer, wished me a happy visit and pottered off back towards the house. I wish I'd known him better.

Visits to Christo were always stimulating and kept you on your mettle (as distinct from on edge!). He would tease mercilessly, but good humouredly, and yet could put his hands up and admit (mostly) when he was being unreasonable. It amused me that he compared the sleekness of my hair to that of Tulipa, his dachshund of the time, and asked if my wife fed me on the same diet of chopped liver and herbs to keep it that way.

He was one of those friends to whom one could talk about anything and everything – from music to writing, plants to people, and, like Oscar Wilde, he seemed to come out with bon mots so effortlessly. I remember regaling him with a story about something I'd written. He looked at me admonishingly and said, "Alan, it's very dangerous when you start quoting yourself."

He did leave me with one lovely tip that has been hugely useful when I can't remember the name of a plant in someone's garden. Christo advised, "Kick it gently with your foot and then casually ask, "What are you calling this nowadays?"

Alan Titchmarsh is a gardener, writer, novelist and broadcaster.

THE HOUSE

One unforgettable evening, Christo prepared dinner for us, the memorable kitchen on view as well. Afterwards, we were led through the private quarters to climb on the roof. The view of the garden from a heightened perspective in the twilight was magical. After we safely made our way back to the drawing room, Christo read to us, thus revealing another dimension of his generous personality.   MARJORIE ROSEN

I sensed at Dixter a timeless quality, one which radiated from the red bricks and tiles of the house and was enlivened by the play of light across the southern aspect of a Sussex ridge. NICOLA MEHDI

It is a great timbered, rambling hulk of a building, this Great Dixter, yet it imposes little on the sublime fields and wood of its gently rolling geology. DAN HINKLEY

The stillness of the house is what I remember from that first visit. You felt it particularly on the landing, coming up the wide stairs in the dark (I never found a light switch – never wanted to) into an unusually big space with Lutyens' lattice work on the side of the stairs, the big window ledge heaped with gourds, wide polished boards underfoot. ANNA PAVORD

Unlike most of Christo's friends, I first became aware of Great Dixter through the writing of his father, Nathaniel Lloyd. I discovered Nathaniel's *A History of the English House* in my school library and it was subsequently checked out in my name continuously for four years. In due course I became a professional architectural historian and without doubt, Nathaniel's book shaped my working life.

In 1987, my partner Christopher Middleton met Christo at Glyndebourne. They got on well and Christo issued one of his invitations to come and stay. At Christopher's request, the invitation was extended to include me. I had a general interest in gardens but my enthusiasm for staying at Dixter owed more to the prospect of seeing where Nathaniel Lloyd had lived rather than to horticulture, although I had read Christo's weekly column in *Country Life* magazine since I was a child.

We arrived on a Sunday in July 1988 with the plan to stay a couple of nights before travelling on to France. Christo met us at Etchingham station and showed us around the public side of the house before a lunch of cold chicken and a salad that included rocket (my first experience of it). Then we had the garden tour and, on that first occasion, we were allowed to ask the names of plants without producing a notebook to jot them down.

We were obviously a hit, because as we were driven back to the station, Christo asked us to spend Christmas with him. Over the years, our friendship deepened and after the sale in 1993 that meant the departure of so much furniture and objects from Dixter, he let me rearrange some of the rooms to hide the gaps. I wrote a new guidebook to the house and published some of my Dixter research in *Country Life*. I'd always admired Christo's writing style and he made sure that if I was to write about Dixter, my grammar had to pass muster. I've always been proud of appearing in the same issue as him.

Charles Hind is H. J. Heinz Curator of Drawings in the British Architectural Library, Royal Institute of British Architecture.

Until Fergus Garrett appeared at Great Dixter, Christo's attitude about the future of the house and garden was, or appeared to be, quite relaxed. "*Che sera, sera*" about summed it up. Then about three years before he died, he decided that he would bequeath his share of the estate to a charitable trust, in the hope that in due course the trust would be able to buy out his niece Olivia, and under Fergus maintain Dixter's traditions and achievements. He asked me to become a trustee, with special responsibility for the house and its contents. As a museum curator, my tendency in 1993 had been to look at old photographs of the house and to put things back where they had been in his father's day. That was anathema to Christo, and I was put smartly in my place. "Put things where they can be appreciated and/or be useful, not just because they were there in my parents' day," he said, and then continued with the clinching argument: "In any case, they were always moving things around themselves, so there is no historic arrangement to return to." A consummate professional in his own field, Christo could teach a professional in another field a lot too!

Dan Hinkley is a plantsman who lives in Indianola, Washington, U.S.A.

Though the skies are clear, there is a stiff southerly that bites to the bones, on this the third of March of 2001 in Northiam, England. Thus the arriving guests dance attendance on the handsome fire that burns in the great hall as they sip their first Champagne. The scene is suggestive of (after my second Champagne) an entire herd on a spit, as they turn in sync to uniformly reheat all sides. In this festooned medieval hall there is a great warmth of camaraderie and much excitement, as we are celebrating a remarkable man's accomplishments during eight decades of life and gardening.

It is the eightieth birthday party of Christopher Lloyd, the imperial wizard in the cult of English horticulture. It was here at Great Dixter that he was born. And it has been through the vehicle of this home throughout his life that he has ignited the jets of horticulture worldwide by a sharp wit and plucky opinion, all the while embracing, as he does still, a youthful vigour in his approach to the garden.

It is a great timbered, rambling hulk of a building, this Great Dixter, yet it imposes little on the sublime fields and wood of its gently rolling geology. Though the manor was first recorded in 1220, the room in which we make merry dates from around 1450. The hammerbeams of oak rise thirty-one feet above, one of which reveals the hollow of a woodpecker's nest. To put this in historical reference, the birds reared their young in this hollow on approximately the same year Machu Picchu in Peru was built.

This piece of writing, however, is not devoted to this house but about this particular day and this particularly remarkable man. Despite the festive atmosphere surrounding this event it is not altogether unlike any other day in this house. Life at Dixter with Christopher, or as much as I have savoured it from time to time, is like a very long and intricately-worded sentence; a synthesis of perpetual entertainment, fine cuisine, opulent plenitudes of Scotch and Champagne and the ratchety barks of ardently pampered dachshunds, all wrapped within an historical house and polymorphic garden.

This afternoon, heaps of heavyweights fill the space beneath the beams – so many enormous names of legendary proportions that I am certain the ceiling will simply lift away. Of course, the heroes and heroines of horticulture are present; but equally well represented are those from literature, music, culinary arts and architecture, a testament to the eclectic, devoted following Christopher Lloyd has drawn to his fold.

For thirty-nine years running, Christopher Lloyd has, on a weekly basis, written a gardening column for *Country Life*. His columns are as spicy and concrete now as they have always been. This while writing sixteen timeless books and countless articles on gardens, gardening and cooking and simultaneously contemplating the responsibilities of Great Dixter. Most amazingly, however, Christo, as he is meant to be called, is an inconceivably gracious host. Not a week or weekend passes in which he does not entertain numerous guests from around the world, offering meals prepared to perfection, while gathering us around his fire each evening for piquant conversation.

Today, Graham Gough, a compatriot from our days visiting the renowned Washfield Nursery, performs Dichterliebe (Poet's Love), a rather broody, fervent poem of a jilted lover by Heinrich Heine, put to music by Schumann. Accompanying him on piano is Pip Morrison, who shared the millennial Christmas with Robert and me at Dixter a year ago. It is a sparkling rendition by both.

On the table amongst bricks of good cheeses is a spring bouquet in colours that I have come to associate with the intrepid aesthetic that Christopher has succoured through-out his career. As I listen to the sublime music, the light from a lovely sunset is spilt upon the arrangement through heavy leaded glass, all while delicious smells begin to waft from the kitchen. After the performance, we rise to sing our birthday wishes and gratitude for this man and he stands for a moment, and then retreats into his study with a charming embarrassment. Now, there is laughter all about the hall while the dogs are creating a fuss in the distance.

Near the end of Heine's poem, the lover finds at long last the sought-for quiet to his unrequited circumstance. In this he has chosen to bury his pain. "And fetch me as well twelve giants, who must be even stronger than strong Christopher in the Cathedral at Cologne on Rhine." I might just say that this Christopher seems quite tough enough.

It was not only gardens that Christo loved. He also had a feeling for man-made things, especially tapestries, woodwork, furniture and pottery. He liked the feel of pots in his hand and above all he liked pots with painted designs and colours, like the great seventeenth-century maiolica bowl, which has a place of honour in the great hall. In his late years he had a particular love of red, yellow and light purple colours and he reorganised some of the beds in the gardens accordingly. These colour predilections also affected his taste in pottery. At the time I had a number of good pots with red and golden lustre. When shown to Christo, he responded to these with his characteristic enthusiasm and acquired many of the best pieces, some as presents for friends, while some (to my delight) remained at Dixter, where they were used or displayed. Amongst them is a flared red lustre bowl, which I would not have parted with to anyone else. Christo gave it a prominent place in the hall.

One autumn day Christo and Fergus came to lunch with us after visiting the Pottery. Though I was looking forward to their arrival, I couldn't help feeling a bit anxious. My garden is a tangled farmhouse garden with an untidy orchard and undisciplined flowerbeds, the opposite of all that Dixter stands for. As we walked around, Christo made none of the critical comments I deserved. Instead, he spotted the quince tree I had planted many years ago, loaded and scented with fruit. "Look, quinces!" he cried out, "You have quinces!" "And so have you," I replied, remembering the gorgeous illustration in *Gardener Cook*. "Not this season," said Christo, "My tree's completely bare." So Fergus and I put up ladders and picked two baskets full, which went back in the car for processing in the Dixter kitchens. My garden had come up trumps after all.

The last message we received from Christo was at New Year in 2006: "Exquisite frost this morning – goose tonight! All good wishes – and look after that quince tree!"

Alan Caiger-Smith is a studio potter who founded Aldermaston Pottery in Berkshire in 1955 and has written extensively on the subject of tin-glaze pottery and lustre decoration.

A photograph sent by Christopher Lloyd to Giny and Andrew Best shows two tables and a lamp by Rupert Williamson and a vase made by Alan Caiger-Smith.

Christo took a great interest in my furniture when he was visiting friends in Scotland. I was told that he turned his chair round so he could study one of my pieces for most of the weekend. With some encouragement from his friends, he asked me to design and make an easy chair and a small coffee table for the solar. Being pleased with the result, he continued to commission work from me for the next twenty years on a regular basis. On his eightieth birthday all his friends clubbed together to commission a table.

We had a businesslike friendship. I would arrive for lunch, which he would cook trying hard to make allowances for my vegetarian taste. We would have a chat about the forthcoming commission before the meal, while sitting in front of one of his blazing fires, or occasionally, if the weather was sunny, on his veranda eating olives and drinking wine (always the best quality). We would have lunch, usually with lovely fresh vegetables from his garden, then coffee in a nice comfortable seat until I realized it was time for Christo's afternoon nap and would leave quietly after looking around the garden.

Rupert Williamson is a furniture designer and craftsman based in Salisbury, Wiltshire.

❧

I first visited Dixter in the late sixties. Christo was away but I introduced myself to his mother Daisy who was weeding in the rose garden wearing her Austrian sunbonnet. Christo's brother Selwyn was married to my then husband's aunt and when Daisy had worked out the connection she greeted me warmly and we chatted amiably about my parents-in-laws' visits to Dixter in the thirties. I bought a *Clematis* 'Lemon Queen' and admired the embroidered furnishings in the great hall which Christo and Daisy had stitched.

Much later in the early eighties I wrote to Christo asking if he would contribute to a book I was planning on enthusiasts for embroidery who were best known in other

Thomasina Beck is an embroiderer and writer whose books on needlework include *The Embroiderer's Garden*.

fields and was pleased when he agreed, "It would make a change from writing about gardening." I was also delighted that he asked me to visit Dixter, "When the time is ripe." The book never materialized but a date was eventually decided on and I set out for Robertsbridge station armed with a small basket, feeling rather foolish as I was uncertain as to whether I was expected for lunch or overnight. "You do travel light," Christo said as he put the basket down by a posy of April flowers in the room I was to stay in. We had lunch on a rug by the horse pond, a large and extremely tough fowl that had been boiled by Christo and carved by his brother Oliver. Daisy's recent death had freed them from the tyranny of cooks and he was just discovering the pleasures of cooking. This was one of my passions and we talked as much about food as flowers on that occasion and continued to do so during our long friendship.

We also talked about embroidery and he showed me the cushions and fire screens he and Daisy had completed using the patterns drawn out for them by the talented designer Dorothy Buckmaster. He lent me a slide of Daisy and himself displaying one of the cushions they had just completed for one of the window seats in the great hall for me to reproduce in my book *The Embroiderer's Garden*. He told me that they had each begun at one end of the canvas and had eventually met in the middle. "Who put in the last stitch?" I asked. "Who do you think?" he replied. He also told me that the first motif Daisy chose to work on a particularly charming fire screen was a brown caterpillar named Sweetie Pie after the current dachshund because of its brown colouring and short legs.

Another vivid memory I have is of a freezing March afternoon with Christo sitting almost in the fire, the only place warm enough to cream butter and sugar for the steamed pudding he had planned to serve during the evening's party. This was also my husband Christopher's first visit to Dixter and Christo invited him to play the piano while he went off to finish the pudding. Time passed and it got colder and darker. Never having sat in this room before I failed to find the light switch and we fumbled our way through the dark house and eventually made it up the stairs to our room. However, the pudding was a triumph!

I first went to Great Dixter in 1941. Quentin Lloyd was then in charge of the Northiam Branch of the Air Raid Precaution and I was a member. Once a week I was on duty for the night at Dixter and we had beds in the great hall. I had driven an ambulance there, a Sunbeam saloon that had been converted to carry two stretchers and had once belonged to Rudyard Kipling. It was a beast to drive as it had a gate change gearbox and very dim lights. Thank goodness there was not much traffic on the roads then owing to petrol rationing.

Christopher and I met as members of Northiam Horticultural Society. He was the President and I was the Chairman for twelve years. Christopher and I remained good friends for fifty years. He gave me a red hawthorn tree and a *Cestrum parqui* so I have a memory of him in my garden. He is greatly missed.

Mary Hartley lives close to Great Dixter and is a member of the Northiam Horticultural Society.

Stephen Rose is an artist.

Christo and I met through the gardener Mark Berry. He had the idea of commissioning a painting of the garden at Great Dixter for his godson, Michael Schuster. Mark recommended me and I drove down for lunch one Saturday in July, after which I toured the garden with Christo. He specified that he didn't want the painting to include the house, but I was reluctant to paint the planted areas as they seemed like works of art in themselves. I suggested the horse pond at the front of the house where we had taken coffee as a good location. The informal planting with its range of shapes, textures and reflected light on the water made it a glorious subject. It also provided a perfect spot to digest one's lunch!

So began an eighteen-month period of frequent visits to Dixter that involved a little painting. Christo had a gift for attracting and developing talent. Among the many visitors were writers, film-makers, basket-weavers, furniture-makers and potters. He enjoyed the company of young people and found them invigorating. Christo also didn't neglect his table and was an accomplished cook. I ate my first globe artichoke at Dixter, copying my fellow diners and arranging the discarded petals around the edge of the plate. I also encountered Jerusalem artichokes and ruby chard for the first time there. The most memorable discovery was the quince with its distinctive scent. We ate it as an accompaniment to some Romney Marsh lamb. There was always consideration given to the aesthetic and organic value of the food in the garden, in the house and on the plate.

Christo could be mischievous. At my first supper, I was faced with a daunting armoury of exquisite, if mismatched, silverware. I selected a pistol-grip fruit knife to cut my pork, as it seemed more up to the job than the knife provided. "Didn't your mother tell you which knife to use?" Christo asked quizzically. Entertainment in the evening consisted of lively conversation and livelier Islay malt whisky. One notable practice was reading to the fellow guests. The short stories of the Edwardian satirist Saki were a particular favourite.

OVERLEAF Stephen Rose's painting that Christopher Lloyd commissioned for his godson Michael Schuster.

Although a noted lover of music, Christo preferred concerts to recordings. Consequently, I only ever heard one piece of music played at Dixter, Janáček's *Cunning Little Vixen*. The absence of television and radio maintained the values of a bygone age of country house entertaining.

The changing seasons brought an end to the public opening of the gardens and the conclusion of my work. Christo and his friends would exchange the drawing room for the solar. These winter quarters were intimate and rich in treasures. On a Saturday in November, lunch was laid out in the solar with Michael and his wife as guests. The finished picture was christened with Champagne.

Great Dixter was a rarified and rich experience for me, one that was pleasurable and formative. I shall always treasure my memories of Christo at home.

FAMILY

My grandmother, Daisy Lloyd, loved sewing of all kinds and excelled at it. Of course, in her day sewing was intensively taught to girls, and in turn she taught it to each of her children, not just to my mother but also to her five boys because as she said, she didn't see why they should grow up half educated.

OLIVIA ELLER

I first visited Dixter in the late sixties. Christo was
away but I introduced myself to his mother Daisy who
was weeding in the rose garden wearing her Austrian
sunbonnet. THOMASINA BECK

We used to take over about twenty singers and artists – if
it was wet, we would have our picnic in the great hall and
if it was dry, we were out on the terrace. All great fun. I
think The Management was around when we first went
dressed in Austrian clothes. LADY MARY CHRISTIE

Christo revered his mother but that didn't stop him
ripping out the rose garden she had planted and installing
billowing cannas, banana plants and his own favourite
Verbena bonariensis in place of the rose garden. PETER FORBES

OPPOSITE The Lloyd siblings from left to right: Christopher, Letitia, Quentin, Patrick, Oliver, Selwyn. ABOVE Daisy Lloyd in puritan dress and her youngest son Christopher display a piece of needlepoint for the camera. BELOW After lunch, coffee was taken by the horse pond.

We had lunch on a rug by the horse pond, a large and extremely tough fowl that had been boiled by Christo and carved by his brother Oliver. Daisy's recent death had freed them from the tyranny of cooks and he was just discovering the pleasures of cooking. THOMASINA BECK

Giny: Christo's love affair with dachshunds spanned many generations – from Sweetie Pie through to Crocus and Sweetie Pie the Second and in more recent times on to Tulipa, Dahlia, Canna and Yucca, the latter two being Dixter's present canine occupants. Christo's dachshunds varied in temperament, though never in their unwavering devotion to him. Tulipa was a notably placid and latterly dignified old lady. Dahlia however was much more volatile and was more than fond of the odd nip. Canna however took a thirst for blood to new levels, and if she took a liking to one's blood her appetite was insatiable. Evening visits to Dixter were heralded outside the front door by wild barking and as one proceeded across the great hall and up the stairs to the solar the barks intensified until the moment when one's courage was plucked up to gingerly prise open the door. The next moment inevitably brought either a sharp nip on my shins or depending on whose reactions were faster, a kick from Andrew which knocked Canna backwards off the first step of the stairs. Christo always serenely awaited us on the sofa and made it his practice to largely ignore tales of blood-letting. Stalemate was later achieved between the warring factions by the wearing of shin-pads as a dress code for Dixter dinners.

For much of his life Christo enjoyed quite a robust constitution as seen in his enormous capacity to enjoy rich food, washed down with copious quantities of wine (his mother Daisy was a teetotaler, except for rum in cooking, so Christo always had to make up for lost time). He also never made a fuss of illness or injury. We were visiting Dixter just after Christo had been diagnosed with cancer of the stomach when a concerned friend rang to enquire of his health. Christo's response to her was, "Well, I'm afraid it's the BIG C," followed by a heavily staged whisper to Andrew and myself, "That'll make her sit up." Appropriate utterings of sympathy were then made by the shocked friend to whom Christo responded melodramatically, "They're going to chop me up – it'll be the end of me!" followed by another

The Best Family

Giny Best is Christopher Lloyd's great-niece. She is married to Andrew Best, and they have three children, Amanda, John and Angus.

side whisper to us, "She loves the drama!" We were then both reduced to helpless laughter which of course infected Christo and the conversation ended with a very worried and bemused friend.

Christo was an amazing host. As our family expanded, he welcomed our new and noisy offspring and even invited us to bring our dogs to stay. Our first labrador Dido first learnt to swim in the horse pond. When she was a little older and more boisterous, to our abject horror Dido ran through the middle of the tulip display in the high garden on one visit. Tulips were torn up and flung from side to side. The result was a devastating battlefield of felled tulips. Christo was silent. He deliberately picked up each and every fallen tulip until he had gathered a large armful and then thrust them into my arms, "They're yours." The retribution was complete.

Being the youngest sibling of six, Christo had grown up in the hurly-burly of family life. At one meal he enquired of one of the children why they were leaving one vegetable aside. They replied that as it was their favourite part of the meal they were saving it until last. Christo roared with laughter. As the youngest in his family he explained his philosophy of always eating the best bits first, lest they be pinched off your plate by an elder sibling. Christo was competitive on every level. Having encouraged and succeeded in getting Amanda to acquire a taste for olives, he would then fight over the few remaining ones in the bowl with her, finishing the tiff with the crowning exclamation of "Mine!"

Christo was a keen practical joker, and if he wasn't practising them himself, he was egging others on with their own. On a sunny day in the summer after lunch, we would transport coffee, chocolates and a rug near the horse pond where we would lie and digest.

One time Fergus and Ken were with us all, and Amanda had taken off her shoes. Quickly one of them hid one of them, and then Fergus found a large stone and threw it some distance into the horse pond, with Ken exclaiming to Amanda, "There's your shoe!" Amanda was confused, while Christo was paralysed with laughter. Fergus' throwing powers were legendary, and were shown off one particularly snowy winter's morning when all the family were on the roof and Fergus was in the sunk garden. Fergus spied us before we spied him and soon there were snowballs raining on top of us, one soaring over the roof much to the admiration of our two boys, John and Angus.

Andrew Best: My first words from Christo were memorable ones. I was standing beside Giny as we stood in a long receiving line at our wedding reception. As the flow of guests breezed past, we heard the following snippets directed at us: "Oh, you look so lovely dear," and "You are a lucky man, you know," with the emphasis on "know". I was getting the hang of it, nodding sagely and smiling inanely and suddenly out of the endless line popped Christo. "I like your face," he said, embarrassing me with his directness for the first time of many. "Come to Dixter," he said, "Ring me when you get back." And with that he was gone. Like many before us, and many after, Giny and I later arrived at the front porch of Dixter to be greeted with a bear hug while the dachshunds were circling at our feet.

One winter evening by the fire in the solar, assembled company were having their pre-supper drinks when Christo's eyes fell on an oil painting of an old man which hung beside the fireplace. "I have never liked that picture," he said. "He has a sinister face and it used to frighten me as a child." Sensible suggestions started to be made (such as to move it out of the way) when another thought was idly proffered. "Why don't you put it on the fire?" Christo's eyes sparkled. After extracting himself from the crowd of dachshunds on the sofa, he flew to the picture and the heirloom was on the fire in an instant. There was a nervous silence all around the room. He hadn't really? He had! Then peals of laughter were heard from Olivia and Giny and although Christo looked slightly guilty, the naughty child had triumphed and had his revenge at last.

Reading aloud by the fire was also something that many of Christo's Dixter guests experienced and I have fond memories of Christo sitting on the sofa in the solar reading, or laughing loudly at funny passages when others were reading. Lots of different stories were read over the years but Saki's short stories were Christo's favourite material as they are far from "safe" – the worst crime that one can be accused of at Dixter. The last time I heard Christo read was by the fire in the great hall when all our family visited during Christo's last winter. His voice was still strong despite his being physically frail and he read to us a story about little Bertha who was good. In fact, she was "so horribly good," that she came to a bad end when her medals for goodness on her chest clanked and alerted the wolf to her hiding place. Christo's emphasis on "horribly good" still rings in all our ears.

On another Dixter visit, the phone rang while Christo was preparing lunch. He listened politely for some time and then made his first excuse. The caller clearly did not take the hint and so Christo said, "I am going to count to three and then say goodbye. One, two, three, goodbye!" The receiver was replaced and preparations for lunch continued without comment.

Amanda and John: Expeditions to Dixter never failed to be eventful. As children we enjoyed many a weekend of infamous Dixter hospitality. On arrival, one was greeted without fail by a chorus of howls from Christo's trusty hounds, lurking menacingly as we tentatively made our way over the threshold. Although the dachshunds were meek and mild in the loving arms of their master, they did not show quite the same affection for the Best family, once forcing Amanda into flight across the long border and into refuge up a near-

Amanda Best on a visit to Great Dixter as a child.

by tree, while John was frequently immobilized with terror at the dinner table when Canna sidled from her corner, strategically nestling herself between John's outstretched legs.

As children, the announcement that dinner was to be served produced mixed emotions for us as although Christo's cooking was unquestionably popular with the older generation, his trademark fish pie did not prove itself child friendly as it was shunted around the plate in vain hope that it would miraculously disappear. However, although we weren't sophisticated enough to appreciate it at the time, fish pie has since become a favourite!

Afternoon activities usually consisted of clambering up onto the roof, games of hide and seek and most infamously water fights with Fergus. As the years passed, this conflict intensified with the use of heavy-duty artillery, which was countered by Fergus and his team who armed themselves with watering cans and hoses. The last battle culminated with Fergus resorting to foul play by fully immersing John in a water trough, with shocked visitors fleeing the nursery, scattering in all directions! Over the years these encounters provided Christo with much entertainment and he greatly enjoyed masterminding a demon strategy to thwart his right-hand man and cause havoc from the safe haven of the house.

Olivia Eller is Christopher Lloyd's niece and the daughter of his sister Letitia.

Dear Christo,

This letter will arrive rather late in the day, but as there are so many things I would like to write about you, it was a job to know where to begin. I have chosen the theme of music, as it played such a crucial role in our friendship.

During one of my visits to Dixter when I was very young, you played me Brahms' waltzes on the Bösendorfer piano in the parlour. The melodies pounded in my ears as I watched your fingers, not the fine hands of an aesthete but strong, gardener's ones, "dancing carrots", as you called them. They nevertheless gave me a memorable interpretation of the pieces. Brahms was there to stay, and you'll be glad to hear that some of his musical scores are still in the house. My interest in music first began in Lebanon where you visited us several times. You went plant hunting with my mother while my father was the patient chauffeur. We played a lot of Brahms on the gramophone there, as my mother was also an ardent fan of Brahms. She had previously not thought much of his style, which was to her all over the place until you explained his music to her, whereupon she changed her mind.

I began grappling with the piano in Beirut when I was four. My mother always brought my piano teacher a thick bunch of long-stemmed violets that smelled heavenly and were neatly surrounded by their leaves. I remember that the keys exuded the smell of some exotic wood. One-handed tunes were so hard to master and a two-handed piece seemed further away than a distant dream. Years later, while I was in the parlour one day before breakfast (as was the custom), practising Bartok's *Mosquito*, you suggested how it should be played just like a real pesky insect that wouldn't go away and your performance was amusing and convincing.

You were chiefly the one who took me to concerts and operas, not just once or twice but regularly so that it became a joyous habit and a feature of the holidays. They were inspiring occasions preceded by an excellent meal somewhere that you had earmarked in town. One of those highlights was watching, for it was quite a sight, Boulez conducting himself in a full Albert Hall teeming with students (there were others but at fourteen I only saw those beautiful, clever people who had such incredible fun); I remember another was when we were sidling out before the end of *Lohengrin* and dashing down to Charing Cross just in time for the last train home with the whole opera still roaring in our heads.

You encouraged me to take up the oboe and so I used

yours, a Louis model, which led to more revelations like Strauss and his oboe concerto. Glyndebourne merits a chapter of its own with comments from the many, many friends you invited. The first you took me to when I was about eight was Rossini's *La Cenerentola*. I wore a new *dirndl* made by my grandmother for the occasion. There were just the three of us, Daisy in one of her long Puritan dresses in heavy grey taffeta with a white tapering collar and Indian shawl and you as a penguin – your rather oddly cut deep plum-coloured suit came later. We sat very near the edge of the stage, quite a treat, and I felt I could reach out and touch the poor maiden in the dust that billowed ochre-coloured in the stage lights.

I also remember having a musical breakthrough when hearing Janáček's *Katya Kabanova* for the first time with you. Sharing our enthusiasm together was something I shall never forget, as well as perhaps what you were all about: keep an open mind, listen and then form an opinion. I would be a lesser person without that.

With love, as ever,

Olivia

Henrietta Leyser is a historian of medieval England, specializing in the history of women and religion.

My late husband, Karl Leyser, came to England in 1937 as a schoolboy refugee from Nazi Germany. It was at Dixter, thanks to the generosity of the Lloyd family, that Karl spent his holidays. To his family in Germany, Karl wrote: "The days pass quickly with reading, various nice games, conversation, music and long, long walks." Karl and Christo were almost the same age and soon became fast friends. Not that Karl was ever converted to gardening. Christo later recalled how Karl had always been "an urban man." When a friend asked him if he could identify a common daisy, Karl said he supposed it was a sort of cow flower. I, too, am no gardener but every now and then I would try to suggest there was still some hope that green fingers might shoot up among the Leyser clan. I remember the occasion when I told Christo that our elder daughter was about to marry a keen gardener. "I suppose he likes sweet peas," snorted Christo. (And so he did.)

I also remember staying at Dixter with my younger daughter and being given free rein in the nursery, where toys and treasures lay still wrapped in the paper and string that had been put around them with infinite care when Christo's sister Letitia first went away to school. On another occasion, I recall sitting with friends among the *Verbena bonariensis* on the terrace and scooping up copious quantities of Christo's avocado dip. I still make this dip occasionally, following Christo's recipe, and on Karl's grave this summer Dixter's *Verbena bonariensis* flourished better than ever before.

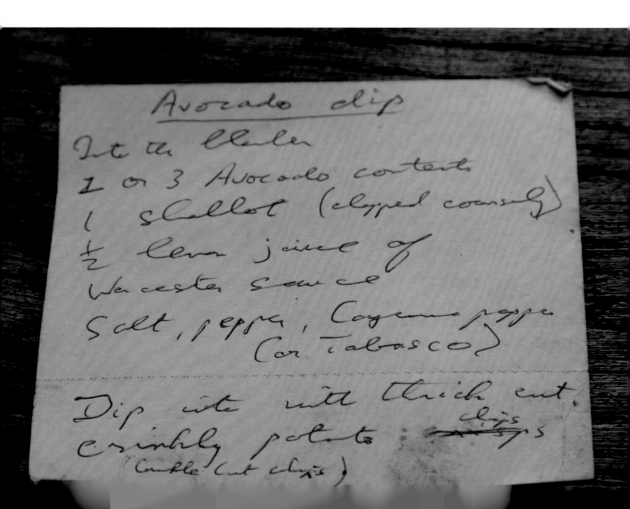

Christopher Lloyd with his nephew
Chris Lloyd in August 1989.
OVERLEAF *Papaver orientale* 'Ladybird'
in the solar garden.

Chris Lloyd is a
great-nephew of
Christopher Lloyd and
brother of Giny Best.

Dear Christo,
I'm such a lousy correspondent – it's been ages
since I last wrote. Not that you have been out of
my mind for a day since we last spoke. Let me see, it's been
nearly three years – it feels like a lifetime.

I can picture you now in front of the roaring fire in the
solar. What might you be doing, writing letters on your old
piece of board? Or, perhaps, like me, you're tapping away in
front of a screen, not on a fancy new Apple Mac like mine,
but on that antiquated laptop running MS DOS WordPer-
fect – the one that I had as a journalist on *The Sunday Times*.
Do you remember? I tried to pass it on to you for nothing,
but it ended up with us having a wrestling match in the parlour because you insisted on giving me £100 for it in cash.
In the end I had to submit. Hand-to-hand combat with my
dear great-uncle, who is forty years my superior, eventually
got the better of me.

Now, let's see. It's quarter to eight in the morning. By
now you'll have walked the dogs, made and baked at least

one loaf of bread (by the way, have you finished all that MacDougall's flour you found in the cellar yet?) and you'll have prepared tonight's steamed pudding for all those guests due to arrive at about six o'clock tonight. Just ten to stay this weekend, I suppose. Standard Dixter fare.

The first time I ever came to stay was when I was sixteen. Someone must have told me (my dear sister Giny, I expect) that you enjoyed whisky. So when I approached the large, imposing Dixter front door, not without a little trepidation, I felt fairly sure that at least I would hit the spot with the large bottle of Scotch I was clutching in my left hand.

But when I presented the bottle of Glenfiddich, with hopeful triumph as you opened the door, your face momentarily fell. "Ugh! You can keep it," you said dismissively, pushing back my outstretched arm, "That stuff's like ditchwater. Come on in, wonderful to see you." And so in I went, still clutching the bottle, and was immediately enveloped by a big bear hug and a long loud laugh.

I wonder how many of your guests coming this weekend will know each other? Not too many, I hope! I have so many fond memories of the five weeks I spent with you, Christo, when I was a student. I stayed in the night nursery, your old bedroom, and helped out Croft with the annual orgy of cutting the grass. "I want this orchard to look like a desert!" I remember you telling me, the day I set to work. Surely this was a chance, I thought, to work off a bit of that puppy fat that seemed to have reappeared during my student days. It wasn't easy work. Raking up a year's growth of grass and forking it up on the trailer was quite a big deal for someone with a suburban upbringing like me.

"Oh Chris, you're not going to leave us so soon, are you?" you'd say (in that tone of voice which meant that saying no was simply not an option), as we headed out towards the horse pond after lunch each afternoon with the coffee and chocolates. "No, no Christo, of course not." I would reply, knowing perfectly well that Croft would have polished off his sandwiches a couple of hours ago, at least.

Staying as your guest that summer meant all those steam puddings and Champagne lunches were bound to take their toll. It should have come as no surprise that despite five weeks of extreme physical exertion, I had actually put on another stone.

But what an opportunity to meet so many of your friends! I kept count – there were twenty-six people in all who came during those few weeks – Colin, Kulgin, Ken, Gill, Damian, Alan Roger, Russ (twice), Nick and Vicky, Frank, Pip, Michael, Pamela Millburn and Beth, to name just a few. Even Paul McCartney! I'm not sure I ever told you about my faux pas that night when Paul came for dinner with Linda. I turned to her, looking for a suitable turn of phrase to grease our lines of communication and innocently asked her if she liked to cook. Well, how was I supposed to know she had her own celebrity line of vegetarian ready-meals!

Then you and Beth plotted to get Paul and me alone together. So there I was, playing the piano in the parlour to Paul McCartney, singing him one of my various homemade songs. What a picture! I have to report that he sat and listened very patiently. I can't quite remember the outcome, but it wasn't quite like how I imagine it must feel to be "discovered." I heard nothing from him again – well, at least I knew then that a career in writing was probably for the best.

You'll probably be having breakfast and taking a look through the post now. Kathleen will have popped in, no doubt, with an update on plans for the day. I'm going to indulge my imagination, just for a moment. As you chat away, I think I'll quietly tuck into another bowl of stewed apple and cream (don't want any to go to waste) and then I'll flick through a few pages of the latest copy of *Country Life*, pausing at your latest articles.

Meanwhile, some steam is rising up gently from a pan of water on a portable stove behind your seat (I can't quite remember its purpose – was it to keep up humidity levels for the plants, perhaps?). To your left is that bunch of blackening bananas hanging on their own mini-hat stand on the table next to the toaster in the corner.

You'll be pleased to know, Christo, that since we last spoke we now have our very own dog. I'm not sure how well Flossie would get on with your two (I'm afraid she's a bit timid), but she's been a complete delight for Virginia, Matilda, Verity and me. We've acquainted her with certain standard Dixter rituals, such as being smothered in a blanket, although as yet she's not shown any inclination to lap up the remains of my cup of black coffee. What are we doing wrong?

Well Christo, it's probably best I sign off soon. I can't tell you how hard it has been not hearing from you these last few years. I badly miss our weekends and your fathomless interest in me each time I call – wherever I may be, whatever you suppose. What's incredible is that you made us all feel that way. Every one of your friends has their own special relationship with you.

Not a day passes when I don't think of you, or see you standing humorously under the "Duck or Grouse" sign in the potting shed. That picture of you, with your eyes twinkling cheekily and your old shoes all hanging out, is stuck on the wall beside my desk. Now I realise what I think I have missed most during the chasm of these last three years – the simple brush of your moustache whenever we kissed hello or hugged goodbye.

The last time we had dinner at Dixter, it was just us two. Aaron was expected back later that evening. I cooked us each a steak and you watched on from a nearby chair in the kitchen, issuing clear, simple instructions. You could hardly walk because of the pain in your knees.

At the end of the meal, you took my hand from across the table, looked me in the eye and thanked me for being such a dear friend. Oh, Christo! How many of us cherish those irreplaceably precious moments we all spent in your wonderful house and garden, one giant family connected only and completely by a deep love for you.

I really must go. Your breakfast may be over; but my day must go on.

Here's one thing I know for sure, even if we can no longer physically speak – you won't have forgotten to sweep up those rubber bands left over from this morning's post. I've got a whole drawer-full myself at home. We're all avid collectors now.

Forever missing you,
Chris

Michael Schuster is a wine writer and lecturer. He and his wife, Monika, are the creators of the Michael Schuster Wine School, which operates as a part of Bordeaux Index in central London.

Christo was my godfather. This relationship was a by-product of the friendship his mother had with my maternal grandfather, Paul Hirsch, whom she first met when visiting the continent in the early twentieth century. The two families became so close that when the Hirsch family left Frankfurt in May 1936 after Hitler's rise to power, my mother Renate, who had been a regular summer visitor to Dixter for many years, spent her first six months in England with the Lloyd family. But apart from a silver propelling pencil as a christening gift, I had no contact with Christo until I was thirty-one. This was mainly because I was born and brought up in Kenya and the families simply lost touch, but he was also uncomfortable with youngsters: "I disliked children because I had no idea what to do with them."

In July 1979 I had a brief letter from him:

Dear Michael,
I've had news of you from your mother in a letter today.... it would be nice to see you properly – I mean not just blowing in and out. Could you come down some time and spend a night at Dixter? Preferably while the garden is still looking nice. I should like that.
Yours very sincerely,
Christopher Lloyd

It was the first of many over the next twenty-five years. And looking on through the correspondence, his personality and interests come across so vividly in his letters, that I thought I would remember him partly through some of them.

For a while after our first meeting in August 1979 we saw each other rarely, but we wrote regularly, because immediately after that initial visit I went to Bordeaux for two years.

Christo was extremely generous in many different ways. Above all he made time – that rarest of commodities today – for his friends. And he took endless time to encourage youngsters whom he felt had talent and energy with help, advice and opinions. He was also very generous with money. He would offer financial help for a new business, buy a suit for someone he felt could do with it but not afford it, not to mention his annual bill for Glyndebourne tickets for friends, which ran into many thousands of pounds. His generosity didn't come from private funds, but from money that he earned. When Monika and I went to visit him in his hospital bed two days after his triple bypass in February 1998, we found him sitting up with his laptop on his knees. "*Country Life* let me know they would cover me until I had recovered," he said, "But I let them know that quite apart from anything else, I need the money!"

Correspondence itself was a notable part of Christo's generosity. "Writing a good letter takes time and effort," he would say. "Most people can't be bothered." But he bothered in abundance, writing letters that were intensely personal conversations: "You have to picture the person you are writing to."

Early on our letters exchanged views on literature and music. As always, he was perceptive and forthright in his views:

Thank you so much for your letter & enclosures Michael. I've not yet broached Hopkins but have

been enjoying and steeping myself in Emily Dickinson who is quite new to me. I started with the ones you marked, and have gone on from there. Although her viewpoint and vision is different from one's own, it is easy to share and identify with them. Her choice of the mot juste is infallible and arresting. She had plenty of time for introspection, but made the most of it.

He concludes with a bit of local colour – he was writing from Alan Rogers' home, Dundonnell House, in Scotland:

I want to pick more rowans to take home for making rowan jelly – excellent with lamb (& venison). I made a start this morning but the rain beat me & now it's streaming down but I think I must risk a wetting!

And later that year:

I've just been steeping myself in Gerard Manley Hopkins, because, wanting to write to you I also wanted to form an opinion, however callow, to tell. What an extraordinary man mixture. Heavily loaded, pushing alliteration beyond the limit; and his vision, his religiosity. Not to my taste, all that & yet genuine, ultimately true to himself & so inevitably to be respected (I wanted to write respectable). Every poem to me is marred ... and yet, and yet (& how he does repeat, maddeningly much of the time) at times, with his ceaselessly uncoiling metre he is effective in so original a way ... I don't think I shall ever be a Hopkins fan but he's certainly worth meeting.

For all his certainty, he was open minded (as above with Hopkins) and prepared to change his views too. In February 2002 I wrote to him: "The English National Opera programme has just arrived. I would love to see *Lulu*, however the director is Richard Jones, he of that ghastly production of *The Ring* we saw, so I can't say I am enthused by the prospect." His response was:

> As regards the ENO. I think we should definitely go to *Lulu*. Richard Jones is at his best with something that is anyway a bit way-out. And he did an excellent production at Glyndebourne of Jonathan Vickers' *Flight*. And when I briefly met him he was both modest and generous about those with whom he had worked. I was disarmed.

His work ethic was famously remarkable. In February 2002 he wrote, "I'm writing, writing, writing. Good weather for it." He was eighty-one! He was so efficient with his own time management (an article before breakfast) that he achieved an enviable balance of work and play, clearly understanding the need for that balance, and indeed the time it required. Writing me a birthday letter in 1980 he noted:

> I did enjoy your visit, Michael. You're a very relaxing as well as stimulating person to be with…. And it's very good for me to knock off (most of) my routine work for a day or two so's to do and talk of something else.

He was naturally thoughtful about the way he related to people, enthusiastically sharing different passions with different individuals.

I went to the opera with him a great deal. He insisted on paying except for the odd occasions when I could plead birthday or Christmas as an excuse. "You book, I'll pay. Seats as close to the front as possible, I'm going deaf." After the performance I would drive him to Dixter, plenty of time to discuss the performance on the way back, and there would be whisky – or tea – with cake or a shortbread biscuit before bed.

His taste was characteristically catholic. In 1982, for example, we went to Loesser's *Guys and Dolls*; Wagner's *Flying Dutchman*, *Siegfried*, and *Götterdämmerung*; Verdi's *La Forza del Destino* and *Don Carlos*; Puccini's *La Bohème*; Janáček's *The Macropoulos Case*; and Strauss' *Salome*. And in 2004 we went to Sondheim's *Sweeney Todd*; Adès' *The Tempest*; Verdi's *Simone Boccanegra*; Puccini's *Tosca* and *La Rondine*; Strauss' *Ariadne*; Janáček's *Jenufa*; Donizetti's *Don Pasquale*; and Wagner's *Rheingold*. The latter was the last opera we went to together. By February 2005, he was writing about the prospect of going to *Walküre* at the end of the month. "I'm not sure how wonky I shall be," and "I find myself increasingly confused, not to say slow."

At a completely different extreme we discovered we had a common interest in reptiles. I collected snakes as a boy in Africa. In the eighties a grass snake, occasionally with its mate, was regularly to be seen sunning itself at the edge of the horse pond on summer mornings. I don't remember seeing them so much latterly, maybe because I wasn't down as often. And for Christmas 1997 he gave me Harry Greene's splendid book on snakes, inscribing it "From one snake fancier to another!"

Occasionally he wrote (in loco parentis?) with concern about my health, with nice juxtapositions about his own:

You're rushing around an awful lot Michael and the sort of life you're leading might be a strain on your heart. I think you should have it checked, just to know where you stand & whether you can continue full steam ahead or – better not.

Any chance of the Madeira coming soon? I'm nearly out of Blandy's and so enjoy a glass before lunch. My cholesterol level is up but I'm still eating Stilton, I'm afraid.

Shortly before he had written:

Christopher Lloyd's recipe book.

I hope you compensate by doing lots of exercises and getting (intentionally) out of breath every day. I do my best to do that, by racing up the Long Border!

He was perhaps typical of his generation in not finding it easy to be demonstratively affectionate, though he became more relaxed about this later in life – a bristly embrace, saying goodbye at the end of a day. But in the opera house, at moments of high emotion, he would reach over, put a hand on my knee and squeeze. That was demonstrative enough for me.

Cuttings from the exotic garden
by Fergus Garrett's desk.

VISITS

I think our lunches were just a little time off from the usual routine for Christo, whereas for me they were always a chance to "get back to the source." I would always drive back to London and my family feeling twice the person who had set off that morning, with a feast of memories and much more to give the world on my return. If, as Emily Dickinson says, "My friends are my estate," then Christo's estate spreads far and wide.   JOANNA BIRD

Visits to Christo were always stimulating and kept you on your mettle (as distinct from on edge!). He would tease mercilessly, but good humouredly, and yet could put his hands up and admit (mostly) when he was being unreasonable. ALAN TITCHMARSH

The cooking at Dixter set trends as much as the garden did. Pink fir apple potatoes, sorrel and rocket were on the Dixter menu a long time before they became fashionable elsewhere. Christo's Sussex pond pudding with a whole lemon in the middle was a triumph. The wine and whisky always flowed freely and on one occasion, a fellow guest leant over and started eating my cheese! At the end of supper, there was a ritual of putting out the candles by holding up your finger and blowing sharply in a certain direction. VICTORIA MILLS

Anna Pavord writes and broadcasts about plants and gardens and is author of many books including *The Tulip*.

The first time I went to Dixter, I was on trial and it felt like it. It was nearly thirty years ago and while working at *The Observer*, I had suggested that the paper should try and bag Christopher as its gardening correspondent. We'd had an initial lunch in London, but on Christopher's side, suspicions lingered. In retrospect I realized I'd been too deferential. It always brought out the worst in him. To an onlooker the worst was often very funny, but I wasn't looking on.

Quite soon after that, a card arrived, inviting me down to Dixter for a night. It must have been summer, because we sat in the yeoman's hall. I slept in the nursery – or rather didn't sleep. There was a full moon: some of the time I lay in bed watching the moonlight's patterns move over the walls of the room, the rest I spent standing by the window, over-revving like a learner driver, looking out at the garden which was filtered by the night into monochrome silvers and greys with long shadows falling over the grass, the topiary dark and watchful. My head nearly burst.

The stillness of the house is what I remember from that first visit. You felt it particularly on the landing, coming up the wide stairs in the dark (I never found a light switch – never wanted to) into an unusually big space with Lutyens' lattice work on the side of the stairs, the big window ledge heaped with gourds, wide polished boards underfoot. You could stand there absorbing the stillness, letting the house enclose you. An ancient cushion-framed mirror on the landing, with misty, opaque glass, was almost my favourite thing in the house.

Mostly I was at Dixter in the winter, when day life was lived in the parlour, the cosy room at the far end of the great hall. I loved this room. In the winter, the fire, built on a great heap of ash, never seemed to go out and in late November, with a cold, drizzly day outside, it was a wonderful place to be. Christopher was one of the few people who still thought Champagne was a good thing to have halfway through a dull winter's morning. He kept a well-stocked cellar and was always generous with it. In that room is fixed a memory of wood smoke, Champagne and Christopher reading aloud. He introduced me to W. H. Hudson and Edward Bunyard, whose book *The Anatomy of Dessert* was a favourite of his. One morning, I was telling him about a friend at whose funeral I had been asked to read some Tennyson. "Read it to me," he said. In the bookcase which covered the far wall, I found four editions of the poems and we spent the rest of the morning reading poems out loud.

Whatever time of day you turned up at Dixter, you pretty much knew where you'd find Christopher. He was like a badger in that respect, his movements round the house following a familiar pattern. There's a kind of groove in my memory that follows a drinks tray through the great hall to the door in the corner, then up the stairs to the solar. This is a magnificent room, running the whole width of the house, with windows at either end and a huge fireplace against one wall. I see it again in winter, the drinks tray (with olives) set on the first table, the lamps on, the fire (even bigger than the one in the parlour) burning well. Christopher was so well looked after by the people who worked at Dixter. The logs were always stacked ready by the fire, always dry. Christopher was usually on the sofa with dog or dogs wriggling about under a blanket. I generally sat to the right of the fire in a wing chair covered in tapestry work that Christopher and his mother had done together. Later, I'd sit on the sofa too, because then he could hear more easily what I was saying. We rarely talked about gardening. Then he'd disappear to cook dinner (always excellent) followed by another procession across the great hall with coffee on a tray. The final ritual was the unpicking of the fire, the remains of logs pulled away from the heart to the edge of the great heap of ash.

I always approached Dixter through the lanes from Bodiam. This way, there was plenty of time for anticipation to build. From the woods, you emerge into Northiam and take the final left-hand turn into the lane that leads directly past

Papaver orientale 'Lauren's Grape'.

the horse pond to the house and its surrounding phalanx of outbuildings. Opening the wicket gate was almost the best moment of all, the porch standing wonkily ahead, the garden familiar, yet always surprising. What might be flowering in the long grass either side of the path? What would Fergus have arranged by the porch? Over the years, the clusters of pots there became ever more outrageous – like Christopher's shirts. No house said "Welcome!" like Dixter did. Nowhere did I laugh more. And that's how I still remember it.

.

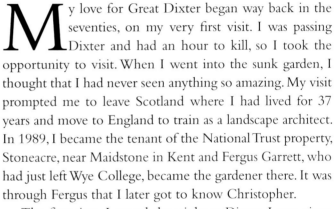

Rosemary Alexander is a garden design consultant and author. She founded the English Gardening School in London, where she remains as Principal.

My love for Great Dixter began way back in the seventies, on my very first visit. I was passing Dixter and had an hour to kill, so I took the opportunity to visit. When I went into the sunk garden, I thought that I had never seen anything so amazing. My visit prompted me to leave Scotland where I had lived for 37 years and move to England to train as a landscape architect. In 1989, I became the tenant of the National Trust property, Stoneacre, near Maidstone in Kent and Fergus Garrett, who had just left Wye College, became the gardener there. It was through Fergus that I later got to know Christopher.

The first time I stayed the night at Dixter, I was given the bedroom that Christopher had been born in. In awe and excitement, I hardly slept all night and read almost all the books beside my bed. Breakfasts at Dixter were always eventful – you never knew who was going to appear next. When Tony Lord or Beth Chatto and Christopher were discussing a plant, the conversation was so scientific that I didn't dare utter a word for fear of being thought a fool. Opening the post was always interesting as well, as people would often send in photos of their plants and ask for Christopher's advice.

We always went round the garden together (I always armed with a notebook, of course), where I was gently teased by Christopher. Once he put an edible flower arrangement comprising mainly of nasturtiums, marigolds and herbs in my bedroom – I considered eating it, but didn't know if confessing that I had eaten the bedside posy would go down well. On another occasion, Fergus took the keys to my car, having told me Christopher would not come out to say goodbye, and loaded it up with plants. I left after break-fast and to my huge embarrassment, Christopher walked me to the car as I was leaving. "Is there ANYTHING left at Dixter, Rosemary?" he asked.

The memories from that unique and warm friendship will never fade.

I will never forget the smell of witch hazel in the chilly air of the great hall, having had the good fortune to spend a number of winter holidays at Great Dixter. Christopher would entertain me with a steady stream of interesting dinner guests and trips to local gardens. When my wife, Sonia, and I were married, we stayed at Dixter during our honeymoon. One night at dinner our charming host poured each of us a half bottle of wine into an enormous glass, saying that once seated he did not like getting up. A man of opinions, he could be curt and to the point. You can imagine his response when I went to the garden to dig turnips and returned with celeriac.

I did not have the pleasure of seeing that extraordinary garden in bloom until 2004 when I brought my son and daughter. After drinks on the terrace and a lovely lunch, Christopher led us on a personal tour. As we explored, he directed the children to provide interference in the throngs of admiring visitors. When I remarked how beautiful the view of the long border was, he said while focused dis-approvingly on a woman with a camera pointed at him, "Sometimes." Rarely did he mince his words.

Tim Brotzman is an American nurseryman who has focused much of his attention over the past three decades on growing quality trees, shrubs and evergreens including his personal favourite, witch hazel.

Hamamelis × *intermedia* 'Pallida'.

S taying the night at Dixter was always a treat. I re-member the feel of bare feet on smooth wooden floorboards on the landing, a huge old-fashioned bath and best of all, the views over the morning garden. Meals were a delicious ritual and after breakfast there was the walk.

The garden was in a constant state of evolution. There were always new things to see, new plants to evaluate and the generous sharing of experiments and experience. Chris-topher Lloyd may have been an old bear at times, and he liked to tease. "Auriculas? We grow them as bedding from seed and throw them away. I can't see the point of idolising them." (He knew I made a thing of auriculas.) "*Hellebores*? Boring..." But to his credit, he was lavish with the sharing of his knowledge and was always open to change and ex-perimentation. He was not a designer, but he was a master craftsman who kept up a constant dialogue with gardeners from all over the world. Horticulturalists sat down to eat with students at his table and to argue about the horticul-tural topic of the day. In the intervals between feasting, they moved outside and worked together in the garden, still talk-ing all the time about why they were doing what they were doing.

One of the most enjoyable and instructive mornings I ever spent was working off the planks in the long bor-der and forking mulch around the plants in March. In Au-gust I watched Fergus inspect some *Aster* x *frikartii* grown from cuttings which were to be planted out at the end of September. In winter, there were snowdrops to admire, al-though they were another plant Christo pretended people fussed over too much. At Dixter the show went on all year round. It was a lively and continuing debate, with everyone invited to contribute. Sometimes I was criticised. I remem-ber asking why some plants were repeated in different areas of the garden. "Well Madam. We must do better for your next visit," I was told. But it was said with such affection that one never felt snubbed.

Mary Keen is a garden designer and writer.

OPPOSITE Looking towards Great Dixter in winter with snowdrops on the ground.

To the young, he was the most encouraging and generous of friends. That many of them ended up with distinguished careers in horticulture is entirely due to the grounding and experience they gained at Dixter. Nor might several young friends have developed such a taste for opera if regular outings to Glyndebourne had not been part of the Dixter way of life.

All of us who were lucky enough to pass through that extraordinary place were enriched by the experience, because Christo was in the end a good and kind man. The first time I met him properly I went down to interview him for an article, just after I had witnessed the death of a close friend in a London street. He said all the right things to a virtual stranger, steering between the perils of mawkishness or callousness, because he understood and was endlessly curious about people. And people, in the end, were what Dixter was, and is, about.

Anne Wambach is a garden
designer based in Sonora,
Mexico.

It's difficult to describe how much Christo's friendship and mentorship have changed my work and outlook over the years – Christo and Dixter have influenced me not only in regards to things horticultural but also in my day-to-day life. I'm definitely a better and happier person for having known him.

In 1983, Christo visited Seattle for the first time to give a series of lectures. One of my horticulture instructors had organized the event and asked me if I would be willing to put Christo up for a few days. He said that Christo had a reputation for being cranky, opinionated and very difficult at times. As I later found out, his reputation was true enough, but these negative qualities comprised only a small part of his repertoire, which also included a remarkable sense of humour and a great deal of generosity.

Our first meeting was a great success, and by the end of it Christo was insisting that I come to Dixter. When I first began to visit, my focus at Dixter was on the garden, but as the years went on, Christo himself became the main draw. He brought people together in the same way he did plants in the garden. You learned quickly that you needed to take his jabs, be able to laugh at them and then counter with jabs of your own. His sense of humour, intense honesty, generosity and diverse interests were like several dear friends packaged into this one great man.

I still hear his voice often, which I find comforting. I was pouring Champagne for a group of friends recently when I heard his firm voice intone: "I like a full glass!"

Opposite Bronze fennel and
forget-me-not.
Right Christopher Lloyd with
Anne Wambach on the terrace.

I have had many memorable visits to Dixter in the twenty-five years since I met Christo. My first was in the month of April when I naively asked Christo "if there would be anything to see," thinking it would be early in the season. I was referring to plants being in bloom of course, which there were in spades. But a garden is so much more than plants. I soon discovered that Dixter was so much more than a garden. Dixter was, and is, a way of life.

Rhythms were as seasonal in the house as they were in the garden, from a drop of scotch by a roaring winter fire to an alfresco summer lunch overlooking the iconic Lutyens steps. The rituals of any day included a balance between work and play. Some days I studied the intricate planting schemes while Christo wrote and Fergus worked in the garden. Other days I pruned roses and cut sweet peas for the house. Tightly woven into Dixter's tapestry were the people whose lives intersected along a garden path or around the dinner table.

One memorable visit occurred when Christo invited me over to help with his then-current book *Meadows*. Christo and I had made several forays to prairies during his travels to Minnesota, and we had shared many botanical and ornithological experiences atop rolling moraines cloaked in native grasses. So, I travelled over to consult with Christo and Fergus on the North American section of the book.

We reviewed Christo's diary notes from his Minnesota visits, recounting a day collecting seeds of *Silphium*, *Eryngium* and *Liatris* with Beth Chatto. Those plants still grow in the grassy swath above the high garden, where Christo planted his prairie treasures. To break up the tedium, Christo, Fergus, Amanda and I took a day trip to the chalky downs near Dover. Christo regaled us with details of the site's ecology, flora and birdlife. He regretfully admitted that he could no longer hear the larks and other birds whose songs are integral to the downs experience.

Working through Christo's diaries was exhilarating and humbling. Ever candid, as he read he never softened his

C. Colston Burrell is a garden designer, author, and naturalist who gardens in the Blue Ridge Mountains in Virginia, U.S.A.

opinions. One day at lunch with Graham Gough and Lucy Goffin, he read not only his notes of prairie impressions from our American tour but also passages about his fears that I was in over my head with a job I had recently undertaken. He read the passage without hesitation, then cocked his head and quietly said, "Sorry, dear Cole." I think his ability to be at once brutally honest and lovingly supportive was what made Christo so dear to his friends.

Our task completed, I reluctantly prepared to head back to Virginia. As I had an early flight, Christo, Fergus and I arose pre-dawn. Still in his robe, Christo walked with us to the car to say goodbye. As dawn illuminated the eastern sky, Christo raised both arms to wave goodbye. With his robe slightly askew and his belly revealed, he looked like Buddha hailing the rising sun. Bathed in an evanescent glow, surrounded by the garden he loved so deeply, he seemed immortal yet fragile. This image is indelibly burned into my mind, and remains one of my most cherished memories

It is curious to me now how few of my memories of Christo and Great Dixter have to do with plants and gardens, when my preoccupation with both are what brought me to him in the first place. As a wide-eyed young student visiting from Wye College, a weekend at Dixter was always exciting; you could never guess who else might be staying, what stories you might be told, what you might experience for the first time. It would often begin with Christo collecting me in his Volvo from Etchingham station; he had an amusing habit of turning off the ignition and freewheeling for as far as he could down the hill that led away from the station – apparently his father could make it several miles without restarting the motor.

To stay at Dixter was to visit another world. There were few modern-day distractions. You felt as if you were glimpsing life from a more elegant age, where the finer and often simpler things in life were celebrated. I was introduced to so much there. Food was a particular joy as my host was a superb cook. It was at Dixter I acquired a taste for olives; Christo kept huge tins of succulent black French ones, which were always a part of his evening drinks tray. I had never been presented with globe artichokes before, but Christo was right, I loved them and still do. I remember one quite delightful summer's afternoon, eating fresh oysters for the first time and washing them down with Champagne on the terrace at the back of the great hall, sitting amid the swaying bells of pink and mauve dieramas.

Evenings could be magical. After a delicious dinner, Christo might lead his guests on a torchlit tour of the garden, perhaps to enjoy the honeyed scent of *Itea ilicifolia* or a flowering ginger in the exotic garden. On other nights we might go up to the roof to look at the stars. In winter my favourite room in the house would come into use – the solar. Here, by a crackling fire, he might read aloud from a book – I remember he enjoyed the short stories of Saki, and he would chuckle as he read or listened.

The gardens of course were an education and often a

Phil Clayton is Features Editor for the RHS magazine *The Garden*.

revelation, yet my favourite spot remains the grassed banks of the water tank at the top of the prairie garden, where on occasion we might have our after-dinner coffee and some Bendicks Bittermints. On a summer's afternoon you can still lie in the sun and listen to the collective hum of grass-hoppers and gaze across the gardens to that lovely house with its towering chimneys, all slumbering in the beautiful Sussex countryside, and simply feel so very lucky to be alive.

Itea ilicifolia by the Lutyens steps.

I had gone out before breakfast to photograph the exotic garden, which looked heavenly in the early morning mist. This was definitely more than ten years ago as I was smoking non-stop at the time. A very kind young man brought me down a cup of coffee and we strolled back to the house and went in via the great hall, when I suddenly realized that I was completely surrounded by wood. Notices requesting me not to smoke were everywhere, and there were also four different doors from which Christopher could emerge at any moment. Predictably, there were no ashtrays. Meanwhile, the ash at the end of my cigarette was beginning to curve down at the tip, threatening imminent collapse. The thought of being found smoking on such hallowed territory was so awful that my only recourse was to drop the offending cigarette into the coffee and drink it.

I particularly remember once describing a flower to Christopher as being violet in colour (I suppose I was just trying to impress by throwing out a fancy name for purple). "Helen, you must learn to get your colours right," he said,

Helen Dillon is an author, broadcaster and garden consultant who lives and gardens in Dublin, Ireland.

LEFT A misty morning in the exotic garden. OPPOSITE *Hydrangea arborescens* 'Annabelle' and *Phlox paniculata* 'Doghouse Pink'.

somewhat crisply. I then asked him to name a flower that actually is violet. "*Tibouchina*," he replied. I always think of him now in late summer when the beautiful Brazilian shrub *Tibouchina urvilleana* comes into bloom.

On another occasion, I was part of a group filming a programme for RTE, an Irish television channel, and Christopher was being very tolerant with all the questions we were asking. Suddenly, there was a yelp of pain from the sound man – one of the dachshunds (I think it was Canna) had taken a good nip at his ankle. "Yes," said Christopher, with a dismissive wave of his hand, "She does that to people she doesn't like." There was no question of an apology or an olive branch being offered and the sound man sulked for the rest of the afternoon.

Later that day, Christopher also pronounced his final damning word on the unsuspecting *Hydrangea arborescens* 'Annabelle'. "She always was a very pushy lady," he announced as we walked by a large plant with especially heavy creamy flower heads.

The first time I met Christopher Lloyd, during an after-hours, late-spring visit to Great Dixter, the chief emotion I felt was pure terror. What on earth would I possibly have to say to this towering god, this wrathful Zeus, of the gardening world, I, an ignorant whippersnapper scribbling away at an American (oh God!) gardening magazine? As it turned out, the only wrath I experienced was from Dahlia, the dachshund (or maybe it was Tulipa?) and even she mellowed after dinner and curled up on my lap. Under that formidable exterior, Christo turned out to be the soul of kindness, guiding me through the garden, answering my appallingly uninformed questions, asking me in turn about my garden and interests. Although we met again several more times, both at Great Dixter and in the U.S.A., that first meeting made the deepest impression on me – evidently, it was possible to be both stern and gentle; to treat gardening with high seriousness as well as a sense of fun; to have strong opinions and yet be willing to entertain dissenting views; to be a world authority on plants and yet insist on taking notes when visiting other (far lesser) gardens. I decided that these apparent contradictions weren't contradictions at all – simply the marks of a rich, complex and fascinating character. Could he be difficult, even rude? I'm sure he could. Was he lovable? Beyond a doubt. Was he a great gardener? A visit to Great Dixter is all the answer that's needed.

Tom Fischer is Editor-in-Chief at Timber Press and a writer of books and articles. He lives and gardens in Oregon, U.S.A.

"I want to get drunk like a Lord," said Christo, inadvertently rendering a perfect visual and verbal turn as Uncle Monty in the film *Withnail and I*. His avuncular tone was admonishing yet jocular and his voice was slightly raised, filling the fire-lit solar as Dahlia eagerly emerged from her blanket and Tulipa growled. My mistake on that perfect Dixter winter evening when I had the old boy to myself was to put out the blended whisky

Edward Flint first visited Great Dixter as a student in 1990. He now lives and gardens in Sussex.

rather than the malt. Christo's hospitality was legendary and it extended far beyond vittles.

Christo gave himself and Dixter to so many, while expecting nothing in return. He infused in me an appreciation of the spirit of Dixter – not the malt, but the sheer joy of gardening for gardening's sake, the pleasure to be had from doing a job well no matter how mundane the job might be. I discovered the pleasure to be had from beady-eyed blackbirds or glistening red admiral butterflies on the *Escallonia bifida*. I remember his delight at the crocus in the front meadow on a perfect Sunday morning in February. He went down on his knees awkwardly to inhale the scent of *Crocus* 'Snow Bunting' while the worthy congregation down the road knelt and inhaled the dust of centuries.

Walking anywhere with him was always an education, something that I could never tire of. Knowledge seemed to filter through naturally with Christo; he didn't teach yet many people learned from him and not just about horticulture. Everything worthwhile seemed to be in his orbit and he wanted everyone else to have it too. He didn't want to share, he wanted to give.

On a side note, in the fifteen years I shared with Christo, I never saw him drunk, either like or as a Lord.

Crocus 'Snow Bunting'.

I wooed Christopher Lloyd for at least seven years, visiting the garden at Dixter as often as I could, before he agreed to write *Gardener Cook*. I had approached him with an idea for a book at an RHS Westminster show, but it was a failure that he teased me about forever.

Beth Chatto eased my first meeting at Dixter as Christo's publisher. She knew I was terrified and took me under her wing, making soothing noises about what a dear chap he was really and how I'd grow to love him. She showed me her room – the large one overlooking the front garden with the cosy four-poster where Christo was born. Little did I know that the posy of flowers by the bed and the click of the door's wooden catch would become familiar. On subsequent visits I slept either in that squishy bed or in the night nursery at the back of the house beneath curving bookshelves packed with Margery Fish. The bathroom down the hall had a basin with enormous brass taps and an enormous tub. Later I found I could lie down in the bath with all thirty-four inches of leg at full stretch. I wondered if neat little Beth and indeed Christo – a giant of a man in my eyes but I had to bend down to hear him – lay under water in that incredibly long bath!

I wish I'd kept a diary of my visits to Dixter. Apart from the books, all I've got to prompt memories are letters, meeting reports and a few transparencies. My photos of the sky reflected in the sunk garden bring back the peace and quiet beauty of Dixter at twilight, but also remind me how Christo had no time for trying-to-be-arty photos. At picture meetings, sitting on piles of cushions so as to look at Jonathan Buckley's images on the lightbox, he would peer through his large, ancient brass magnifying glass (which always needed a surreptitious clean) and reject anything that didn't have editorial value. "Focusing on the flower doesn't show the plant's form," he would complain. Recollections of sitting with Christo by the fire in the parlour merge with similar memories of after dinner in the solar, one dog lounging on the floor, another wrapped around his neck.

Erica Hunningher is an editor who has been the creative force behind a host of gardening classics.

OPPOSITE FROM THE TOP
Narcissus bulbicodium var citrinus;
Tagetes 'Cinnabar'; *Dahlia*
'Moonfire'.

Now and again, Christo would get up and practically disappear under the huge fire to add a log. Some evenings I also sat in the parlour on my own, eating black olives and sipping sherry, while he had his bath and put the supper on. He'd come back with a timer and quiz me on what I'd been reading. I once made the mistake of telling him I'd come across a word I didn't know in the *Literary Review*. "You can look it up after we've eaten," he said, "There's a dictionary in the solar." He giggled surreptitiously during dinner, his chin almost touching his chest, and, of course, the word turned out to be an embarrassing one I should have known and Christo gloated on my ignorance. (On the other hand, he was an encourager and one St Agnes' eve showed his delight that I was able to rattle off some Keats.)

Christo was generous with praise (I treasure a chapter of *Succession Planting* which is inscribed with a note, saying, "I think you have markedly improved this chapter. Don't make a habit of it, though!"), but he never forgot something that displeased him, even if he could forgive and laugh about it afterwards. He was livid with me when his agent, Giles Gordon, reported that I'd got the green light to go to contract with him and Beth for *Dear Friend & Gardener* on condition that they wrote to each other mostly about matters horticultural. (The sales department considered Glyndebourne to be elitist.) Thank heavens the two friends set about ignoring this caveat – writing plenty of exchanges on the opera, as well as cooking, music, birds and the night skies – and Christo set about reminding me of its stupidity as often as possible.

Christo's powers as a writer never dimmed but he did get tired. Fergus kept him on the *qui vive* to finish each book and for some of the *Meadows* and *Succession Planting* captions I took dictation. "Remind me why we put these pictures here," he'd say. "Ah, yes. How many words?" I'd give a range, from sixty to eighty words, say. There'd be a pause and then he'd start and continue to the end without stopping – an entire thought process beautifully expressed and constructed without a hitch.

It was at lunch with Colette Foster, one of the producers for Gardeners' World, that I finally got my own back over my initial failure to "get" Christo. "When I first met Erica," he told Colette, as we cleared away the pudding plates, "she made this ridiculous suggestion that I should write a book called 'The Provocative Gardener'. Of course, one doesn't set out to provoke." There was a pause. "I should have suggested 'The Bad-Tempered Gardener,'" I mumbled bravely. "Would you like some cheese?" Christo asked Colette, adding with a wry grin, "I'm not offering any to Erica."

Some years ago, I was one of a gaggle of hardcore gardeners en route to a symposium, "A Week in the Garden with Christopher Lloyd". I was more than a little apprehensive as I was about to meet my gardening hero, a man whose brilliance, facility with language, and failure to suffer fools gladly – or otherwise – were legendary.

It has been stated to the point of trivialization that Christo gardened to shock. Perhaps, but more than that he loved the "Gotcha!" moment that is at the heart of good music and good jokes. He loved word play, and was quick to recognize fellow gamesters. You could (almost) always tell when the game was afoot. There would be an almost imperceptible quickening, a frisson in the tempo of the conversation as Christo gathered his audience to him and then... Gotcha!

His sense of fun could be quite basic. In his later days, he looked at his feet as he walked – especially on stairs. I was once working near one of the staircases and made the mistake of greeting him unawares. He was, I'm afraid, rather startled. About thirty minutes later, when I was thoroughly stuck into pruning a fuchsia, I was startled out of my skin by a loud "Boo!" in the vicinity of my left ear. Christo, eyes alight with mischief, had gotten his revenge.

Kyle Landt is a keen gardener and an Assistant Professor of Pediatric Endocrinology at Dartmouth College in New Hampshire, U.S.A.

Christopher Lloyd prepares for a bonfire.

Another day, another staircase. I was back at Dixter for the first time in almost a year. I was moseying down the Lutyens circular stairs, alone – or so I thought. There, in what had been a rather worn grass rondelle, was the most amazing, outrageous, magnificent collection of succulents. I could only give voice to my reaction in the vernacular of my generation, "Far freakin' out!" From the vicinity of my right elbow purred a very familiar and much beloved voice, "I was hoping you would think that, my dear!" Gotcha!

"What are you doing this summer?" Oliver Lloyd asked me. We had become friends while both studying music at Bristol University. I shrugged. "I'm going to visit my brother for ten days in Sussex and wondered whether you would like to come with me. I'm not keen on driving all that way by myself and I have two tickets for Glyndebourne to see *Der Rosenkavalier.*" No further persuasion was needed. Oliver knew that I loved Strauss and had never been to Glyndebourne. Despite the forty-year age gap, Olli and I became good friends. We were both passionate about composing, art, history and architecture.

On the journey to Sussex, Olli told me a little about where we would stay. To my horror, he informed me that it was hundreds of years old – I remembered the mess that he had achieved in just thirty years in his Art Deco house and wondered what his bachelor brother was capable of committing in a relic! He also said that there were extensive gardens that had been laid out by the family.

As we clocked up the miles, my initial excitement at spending a week in Sussex increasingly turned to dread. After many hours we turned off a village road and entered a narrow drive, parking outside Great Dixter. "Here we are!" My surprise was total as people came to greet us and take in our bags, referring to Olli as Mr Oliver. Naturally I fell in love with Great Dixter immediately; Olli's brother Christo was a different matter.

From the beginning I was aware of a sibling tension. Conversations were polite between them but peppered with references to past events or characters whose significance was never explained to other guests. They seemed much more at ease with each other when wandering around the immaculately kept borders discussing the plants. "Oh, I have one of those at home," Olli would say. In my mind I would picture his overgrown jungle of a garden and wondered if his brother imagined the same scene.

Russell Pascoe is a composer and Director of Music at Richard Lander School in Cornwall.

On returning to Cornwall, I realised that I had left my wallet at Great Dixter. I phoned and asked if it could be sent to me. Weeks later an envelope arrived with a handwritten white card. "Nasty Remains. Christo."

A year later, Olli asked me to accompany him again and repeat our trip. I told him that I didn't think that his brother liked me very much and quoted the contents of the card. "Mmm! That's very naughty of him. That was a saying of our mother. He shouldn't have used it outside the family. You must come. Christo is looking forward to seeing you. He thought you charming last year!"

One day, on my birthday, I answered the phone to Christo. He had never called before and I wondered how he had got my number. "What timing! It's my birthday!" I gushed. "Oh. Happy birthday!" he replied. "Did you know that Oliver is dead?" "What? No! How? When?" I was obviously very shocked and upset. The news came as quite an emotional blow as I was leaving my house for an evening of celebration. "Don't get all sentimental and mawkish! We buried him last week. You couldn't have cared that much about him! When did you last contact him? His body lay undiscovered for several weeks. The alarm was raised when he failed to turn up to chair a meeting of the Speleological Society. Do you still want to come to Great Dixter this summer? Oliver bought you a ticket for Glyndebourne and it will only go spare."

This conversation was typical of the Lloyd sensibility! Over the years, I realised that if someone died or had fallen out of favour, they were never referred to again. Countless people who had been guests at the house were simply obliterated in this way. Likewise, I noticed that after a robbery at the house, in which precious heirlooms were stolen, a similar pragmatism was displayed. This also extended to the garden. "You mustn't get sentimental about plants!"

In the years that followed Oliver's death, Christo and I became good friends. Every Christmas, he would phone me up and invite me to choose which opera I would like to attend. He knew my taste: Strauss, Monteverdi, Janáček. The only year I wasn't invited was the all-Mozart season. "It would be a waste of money," he told me. I must have said something disparaging about the great man at some point. Generally our tastes were similar, though he disliked Tchaikovsky's *Eugene Onegin*. He could also be dismissive of some of my favourite operas by Benjamin Britten. We both agreed on Strauss and would spend evenings in the solar enjoying his operas.

In 1999 my opera, *The Murder of Charlotte Dymond*, was to be performed in Truro. Christo had stayed with me on several occasions and loved the fact that I seemed to know everyone in the town and that, as a teacher, pupils would greet me with, "Alright, Sir!" I had decided to dedicate the opera to him. I'd always found it impossible to know what to get him as a present and an opera, for the man who had taken me to so many amazing productions, seemed the ideal gift.

Despite the fact that he had a book signing in London the morning after the first performance, Christo made the long journey to Cornwall with Fergus, Amanda and Stephen. The night they arrived, I took them out for a meal. Having my Dixter friends visit for the premiere made the occasion even more special and exciting. They were staying in a "Fawlty Towers" bed and breakfast and regaled me with stories of their ludicrous experiences.

I think that Christo enjoyed his opera, but as soon as it was over he and our friends made the long trek home. Afterwards, he would beam with delight as he remembered how as we took our seats in the theatre, someone shouted out my name. As he and I turned around, at least fifty people stood up and waved. Everyone laughed. Christo didn't like parochialism, but he loved the fraternity of friends.

After he died, we went to Glyndebourne and drank Champagne in his honour. We lit the smoke bush, ate sandwiches carried in the old wicker basket and sat on the same rough rugs. Our conversations, however unconnected,

Ox-eye daisies in the foreground with topiary in the peacock garden.

naturally meandered back to memories of our friend. But we were not sentimental or maudlin. That was the last thing our host would have countenanced.

Christo announced one morning that we were to have peaches for a morning treat. A ladder was taken into the walled garden and propped up against the wall-trained peach and up he went to pick two peaches. "Hmm," he murmured as his big hand darted among the fruits. His shoulders were quivering as he shouted down, "Are you ready?" I got ready with cupped hands to receive the first peach. I am hopeless with ball games, especially when catching is involved. Nevertheless, I went into action as the thrown fruit came down at me. I caught it first time! Then I immediately threw it back up in the air. On its journey down, it had a wasp as passenger! It must have been as surprised as I was. Christo was up the ladder giggling, very pleased with his selection of an inhabited peach just for me.

Ken Rawson met Christo in 1986 and is now a garden designer based in Lincolnshire.

Coffee by the horse pond May 1994 (left) and picking peaches September 1987 (opposite).

Christo was nothing if not mischievous and he sometimes had such a restrained way of playing a little prank, with his head slightly bowed so you missed the spark in his eye, that until you knew him better you wouldn't believe such mischief was really in him.

After he'd given my first book on annuals an enthusiastic review in *Country Life* – I think we were both overjoyed to find someone else actively interested in annuals – he invited me down to stay at Dixter. In the evening we sat by the fire with the dachshunds, looking at books and catalogues, talking about plants and enjoying the cosy warmth. He eventually retired to bed but I stayed on – just enjoying the atmosphere of the place.

When I too became bleary I opened the door to make my way upstairs to bed – and found the whole house in complete and utter darkness. He'd turned off every light. Finding my way back to my room through the rambling house with its two staircases might have been possible if, having not closed the door on the embers behind me, I could see a wall or a door or my hand in front of my proverbial face. But as it was, I could see nothing.

What could I do but set off in what seemed – clunk, I hit my shin on one of those ancient oak chests – in what seemed like the right direction. Twenty-five minutes later, with the help of a little moonlight gleaming through an upstairs window, I finally found my room and was able to massage my bruised shins. I never did locate a light switch.

Finally tucked up in bed – who knows where the bathroom might have been – I looked around for reading material. I always like to read before dozing off and I thought that at Christopher Lloyd's Dixter, of all places, I'd find something interesting. A single shelf ran along the wall above the bed – it held a seemingly endless run of the Proceedings of the International Plant Propagators' Society. In spite of my bruises I was soon asleep.

Graham Rice trained in horticulture and botany at The Royal Botanic Gardens, Kew, and is the author of numerous books on plants and gardens.

David Wheeler founded the horticultural journal *Hortus* in 1987 and is one of a small team of writers who filled the gap in *Country Life* following Christopher Lloyd's death.

Distance, more than anything else, prevented me from joining Dixter's inner circle. Convivial weekends are part of the Dixter legend, but since starting *Hortus* I have lived in Wales and then in north-west Herefordshire, some two hundred miles from Northiam – a distance that precluded short bursts of regular social gallivanting in the south-east of England.

But Dixter was very much on my radar, as it was on that of so many other gardeners with their ears and eyes on the ground. Who could ignore Christopher Lloyd's weekly succession of *Country Life* articles? Which of us has not learnt from his many books? Along with Beth Chatto's *The Dry Garden* and Robin Lane Fox's *Better Gardening*, Christopher's *The Adventurous Gardener* was among my bedside comforters and inspirations during my early London bedsit days, when a large house and garden in the country was no more than a seemingly impossible dream.

Later, in 1999, I asked Christopher Lloyd if I could come to Dixter to talk about his involvement in the gardens at Glyndebourne. He too was a keen opera-goer, and having just been asked to write a book about the gardens surrounding the Sussex opera house I wanted his take on the shaping and reshaping of its few famous downland acres.

Typically, I was asked to lunch. It was a bleak early spring day, a day cheered outside by a galaxy of naturalised crocuses on the lawns flanking the path to Dixter's gabled porch, and brightened inside by a blazing log fire and a bottle of sherry in Christopher's small sitting room. We ate olives, sipped the sherry greedily and exchanged stories (many featuring our mutual love of dogs) before I was asked to amuse myself while he prepared lunch in the kitchen.

Somewhat surprisingly (as no one else joined us for the meal) we ate in the dining room, sitting opposite each other in the middle of the modern (and then newly installed) long table. Details of our conversation have faded over the years, but I will never forget the turbot that had been so skilfully poached in my honour. "Landed this morning at Rye," I was

assured – succulent, gelatinous, smelling and tasting of the sea, washed down by a costly Chablis that might have been chilled on a frosty north-facing doorstep.

After lunch we retired to deep armchairs in the sitting room for coffee and chocolates. Christopher drew a blanket over his knees while two of his much-loved dachshunds served as muffler and scarf. We chatted on seamlessly, until the warmth of the room (not to mention the sherry, the white wine and probably my mind-numbing ramblings) induced a closing of Christopher's eyes. His deep snores were soothing, perfectly in tune with those of his dogs, and he slept peacefully for a quarter of an hour or so, until I all too noisily added more logs to the fading blaze. "Would you like a cup of tea before you leave?" he asked as he woke. "Or a stroll in the garden? Not [lying of course] that there's much to see at this time of the year."

My only regret is that I could never persuade Christopher to write for *Hortus*. One of his several letters in reply to such a plea says, "I doubt you could pay me enough. I have a very large roof to keep up." Proof, if proof is needed, that he was as astute about matters financial as horticultural.

As I write this, Christo's photograph sits on my bookcase and *Cuttings* is on my reading pile. Christo and Great Dixter are always with me, as are the memories I have of living and working at Dixter during the nineties and more recently. Dixter is not just a place, but also a way of life that became part of all the people who shared in it. It was the little things and everyday occurrences that made it so special. There was no radio or television to distract, just a focus on life, people, plants and nature. Those who were part of Dixter will understand the expression of feeling "dixtered" – a sense induced by trying to keep up with Christo's seemingly inexhaustible energy that left one feeling somewhat depleted when it was time to leave.

Brent McKenzie trained as a gardener in Dunedin, New Zealand in the late seventies and now runs his own garden design and consultancy business.

Hedychium densiflorum
'Assam Orange'.

I first met Christo on his visit to New Zealand with Beth Chatto in September 1989. His insistence on meeting me caused the organisers of his speaking tour to invite me to stay as their guest. He came again to New Zealand as our guest on another sell-out speaking tour.

Seeing Dixter for the first time was still clear in my mind some two years later. I was collected from the London train at Northiam on a grey November morning and as I was driven down Dixter Lane, the house seemed to rise up out of the ground as if growing in front of me. It's a memory that never ceases to stir me.

How did this all happen? I purchased a copy of a book called *The Adventurous Gardener* by a chap called Christopher Lloyd and finally read it over a wet Christmas. While reading it, I nodded in agreement and laughed out loud. After finishing it, I found an address for the author, wrote to it and was surprised to get a handwritten reply (which needed some deciphering). This is what it said:

Dear Mr McKenzie

Thank you very much for your letter and for conveying your enthusiasm for my *Adventurous Gardener*. That gave me a lot of pleasure. It's so much commoner to write when one violently disagrees. When you're pleased you think (not often) "Yes, that was good, I ought to write," but nothing happens. (I do it myself, but not always; I once wrote to the sports correspondent of the *Financial Times* to say that, although I haven't the slightest interest in sport and am a complete duffer at any sort of ball game, I always read his contributions because he made them so interesting, even to me. He was pleased.)

Perhaps you'll do me the compliment of reading something else by me.

[In reference to an advertisement that I had enclosed.] I was amused by the Buddleja 'Royal Red' and also by the one beneath for "a soft pink" lavender.

It is a horrible dirty non-colour! Well they have to sell the plants.

Actually, I do run a small nursery but only of plants I like and respect. I'm a poor salesman of those I don't believe in.

You know more about me, Brent McKenzie, than I do about you. If it wasn't too great a bore to write me something about yourself, I shall be interested. There's a great bond between plantsmen gardeners, wherever they may be.

Whether you write again or not, thank you for your letter. If you come to England, ever, you must visit Dixter.

Yours sincerely,
Christopher Lloyd

Such amazing memories. Thank you, Christo.

The cold frames with the potting shed in the distance.

As a weekend visitor to Great Dixter, I always looked forward to the moment when Christopher Lloyd would say, "Let's go and see what the girls have been doing." Although Sissinghurst's controlled colour schemes were not to Lloyd's taste, interesting changes in planting and clever combinations would be recorded in his notebook for possible use at Dixter, albeit with slightly more punch.

Tony Lord is a horticultural author, editor and photographer.

Dr Brent Elliott is Historian to the RHS and author of numerous articles and books.

I first knew Christopher Lloyd through his books. When I first became engrossed in garden history, on arriving in England in the seventies, the first modern gardening books I acquired were Graham Thomas' *Perennial Garden Plants*, and three of Christopher's works: *Clematis*, *Foliage Plants*, and most importantly, *The Well-Tempered Garden*. This latter has remained for me the best of modern gardening books and the one I return to most frequently and recommend to others who are making their first explorations of the subject.

I first visited Great Dixter in 1976, but did not meet Christopher until well into the eighties. He hardly ever visited the Lindley Library in London; the literature he needed for his work he had on his own shelves. I saw him most regularly at Chelsea lunches, where I usually sat at his table and was treated to his comments, occasionally acerbic and not exactly sotto voce, about the officials and other dignitaries who made speeches.

The main impression of Christopher in my memory is of his restless curiosity and his willingness to experiment with aesthetics and techniques before making up his mind.

Jean Elliott and her late husband Jack were regular visitors to Great Dixter from their home in Coldham, Kent. Jack Elliott was a past President of the Alpine Garden Society and author of several books.

It was always with the greatest of pleasure that Jack and I accepted Christo's invitations to Great Dixter. Many happy moments were spent exploring the beautiful gardens, talking about the plants, and sometimes even being critical of the colour schemes. This was inevitably followed by a delicious meal and carefully chosen wine. On several occasions Christo came and had dinner with us at Coldham, latterly accompanied by Fergus, who would drive him over. Jack was always on his guard when discussing anything in the garden. On one occasion I remember a rather facetious remark was made about something that Christo had noticed and before you could turn around out came the little black book and within a week the remark was in print in *Country Life*! Happy days.

Christo was never very good at sports. With real hatred in his voice he would tell me about being forced to play cricket at boarding school. But he was rather good at passive sports. He was a good shot, for instance. At the time when I lived in Garden Cottage at the far end of the nursery, sometimes on summer mornings I would be woken up by gun fire. That would be Christo shooting the rabbits that were nibbling at the young clematis plants. He used a .22 rifle instead of a shotgun and seldom missed. He loved the sound of the hunt in winter when the baying of the hounds would echo through the valley. He allowed hunters to charge all over the estate. One year, a fox sought refuge in the long border and the pack of hounds charged all over the garden. I thought it was hilarious but Christo was not amused. There were no more hunts on Dixter territory after that.

The winters were long at Dixter. The garden was closed and as the heating system of the house didn't function very well, friends would stop coming between autumn and spring. Christo – whose friends were mostly elderly in the seventies when I worked at Dixter – felt that he could not offer his guests enough comfort. One sport, if I may call it that, which Christo excelled at was chess. When I think of Dixter, I think of the long winter evenings spent in front of a roaring fire in the solar with Christo, drinking whisky, discussing all sorts of big issues, and playing endless games of chess. I lost more often than not.

Romke van de Kaa was head gardener at Great Dixter from 1976 to 1979 and is now a horticultural writer.

CHRISTOPHER

A fundamental memory
Christopher sitting
Partially slumped
Eyes hard to detect beyond the horn-rims (and impossible
to detect when snoozing)
And then, that glorious sparkle from within him, articulated
from his lovely light blue eyes shining above the rim of his
glasses.

GEOFFREY DYER

That he wanted to add orange rind to Delia's Chocolate Squidgy Log recipe is something of a metaphor for all his relationships. Michael McCoy

After dinner the Milky Way was clear in the sky and there were shooting stars. I don't think I'd ever seen a shooting star before that evening. How fitting that my first sight of one was at Dixter. Christo blazed his own trail – as a singular teacher and as a man who loved plants, the arts and good food. He was a whole planetary civilisation in himself, one which we satellites were happy to orbit. Peter Forbes

Christo's style was entirely different – open, imaginative, innovative, impish and inclusive. John Sales

The phone rang while Christo was preparing lunch. He listened politely for some time and then made his first excuse. The caller clearly did not take the hint and so Christo said, "I am going to count to three and then say goodbye. One, two, three, goodbye!" The receiver was replaced and preparations for lunch continued without comment. Andrew Best

I loved Christopher Lloyd's writing and thought he was just the funniest, best author ever. You could enjoy his books even if you didn't care the first thing about gardens or plants. Helen Meadors

Beth Chatto and Christopher had been friends for a long time, but until one Saturday morning not long before he died, I had never seen them together, although I had photographed both of their gardens for several years. That Saturday, I was working in the tropical garden at Dixter and heard him say, "Is Jerry there?" Christopher appeared around the yew hedge, followed thirty seconds later by Beth, holding a Japanese anemone.

Jerry Harpur is an international photographer of plants and gardens.

Hugh Johnson is a British author who has written classic works on wine, gardening and trees.

Christo had no especially high opinion of my skill as a gardener, but like all possessors of good wine cellars he liked having fellow addicts around to discuss his wine with.

He brought up some pretty respectable claret when Judy and I went to Dixter, (trugfuls of vegetables are my principal memory of the immense kitchen), and I dug fairly deep in the cellar on the occasions when he came to see us at Saling.

It is not his reaction to my wine that I remember, though. It is the discerning eye that told him at a glance that I was a rank amateur in his profession. I was rash enough, I remember, to draw his attention to some plant that I considered rather a success, and will never forget his response. "Ah yes," he said, "We start by thinking all our geese are swans."

I have been tempted to quote him many times when someone has invited my admiration for a Bolivian Chardonnay or Albanian Pinot Noir – but a true professional is ruthless, and I'm a patsy.

Joy Larkcom is a writer, broadcaster and gardener who is especially knowledgeable about vegetables.

When I think of Christo, he's standing by a flower bed, head tilted with that slightly impish look, delivering one of those unforgettable one-liners: "Everybody has a *Meconopsis* phase," "What's the matter with clashing colours?" and memorably, on his first visit to my garden, "I always knew it would be a mess." He was always fun to be with, perceptive, unbelievably generous with knowledge, hospitality and encouragement – and gloriously gossipy. People and plants vied for his interest.

What a legacy he left. So many of the plants I grow, see, or would like to grow, I first encountered at Great Dixter. In my memory, they are imbued with Great Dixter vitality. That same vitality springs from Christo's treasured books and articles. It will never pall. I hate to think there will be no more additions to my "Christo article" file.

I treasure the last typically bubbly letter he wrote to me, after a visit to Ireland. "You're amazingly positive, but have never quite received the recognition for your original work that you deserve. You seem happily resigned to that." I include this snippet not out of false modesty (I was very touched), but because it was so typical of Christo, illustrating his unfailing urge to encourage, to give credit where it was due, and to help fellow gardeners and writers in any way he could.

I am wincing a little as I write this, but I think it's fair to say that Christopher and Dixter changed my life. As a sixteen-year-old with an already substantial interest in horticulture, I thought I was destined for a biology or biochemistry degree followed by a life in a white coat in some laboratory splicing or unsplicing genes or something similar. But then a copy of Christopher Lloyd's *Foliage Plants* arrived from a book club – I read *The Well-Tempered Garden* immediately afterwards. Before long, my interest in white coats began to wane.

What was so special about the books, the man and the garden at Great Dixter? I had read many gardening and plant books previously, but at best they generally added to what I knew but did not inspire, provoke or challenge. Lloyd's books were different: intensely personal, provocative, full of verve and wit. They suggested that there was an intellectual culture somewhere within the horticultural world that I hadn't previously fully appreciated. My careers teacher had not read either of these books and was not amused when I announced to him that I was going to apply to do a degree in horticulture.

My first contact with Christopher was during my PhD when Great Dixter became one of the sites from which I gathered information on how plants that are difficult to grow respond to winter cold and insufficient summer heat.

James Hitchmough is Professor of Horticultural Ecology in the Department of Landscape at Sheffield University.

Christopher filled in yet another of my interminable questionnaires a decade later, this time on his experience of establishing cultivated herbaceous perennials in garden meadow grassland. We bonded over this latter interest, probably because there weren't many others around who shared this somewhat niche pursuit.

As I got to know him better, what I really admired about Christopher was his capacity to deal with radically new experiences, despite having spent most of his life in that house on the side of that hill. When researching the chapter on creating meadows for his book of the same name, I organised for him to meet Richard Scott of Landlife to look at some very wild meadows in parts of inner city Liverpool. He coped with the burning and burnt out cars that are sometimes an occupational hazard in inner city meadows without batting an eyelid. Perhaps this was old school grit, but I personally think he retained the capacity to constantly re-imagine the world and himself to the end. So that's pretty much it. Christopher, I never told you of your seminal influence on my career; but thank you for writing those books.

Below left to right: *Crocus vernus* naturalized in the meadow; Coleus on a bench in the greenhouse; *Plectranthus argentatus, Anaphalis margaritacea, Aster* 'Little Carlow', *Rudbeckia fulgida deamii* and *Miscanthus sinensis* 'Strictus' in the high garden in autumn; crocus and narcissi in the meadow entrance.

Christopher Middleton is
a pianist, conductor
and vocal coach.

Christopher Lloyd at home
(opposite) and with friends at
Glyndebourne (below).

Christo and I first met at Glyndebourne and that is where I saw him for the last time at a performance of Mozart's *The Magic Flute* the summer before he died. Music brought us together and it was music that made us friends; he was one of the few non-professional musicians with whom it was a delight to talk about music – his understanding of it and especially of opera was profound and particularly relevant to me as a vocal coach. We shared a passion for Wagner and Janáček and had many long discussions about *Tristan*, *Meistersinger*, *The Ring*, *Jenůfa* and *The Makropoulos Case*. I never did succeed in coaxing him to the piano to play any duets, but it gave him much pleasure when I would bring down any scores I was working on to Dixter and the strains of Isolde's curse or Wotan's narration would waft from the parlour's Bechstein into the great hall. Unfortunately these occasions brought less pleasure to the long-suffering house guides who were deafened by the music while attempting to address their flocks.

I had never heard of Christo or Dixter when we met, which was probably just as well as I would have been intimidated and we wouldn't have clicked the way we did. I soon learned not to ask for plant names as we walked round the garden – "There's no point in telling you, you'll just forget if you don't write it down." However, as I gradually gained some knowledge and was able to ask the occasional at least partially intelligent question, or even challenge one of his more eye-watering colour combinations, he would mellow and respond warmly. When Charles Hind and I eventually acquired our own relatively tiny garden he came to see it and pronounced it "Fun," which is a compliment we both still treasure. I wish it had not taken us a further twelve years to follow his advice and remove the patchy grass and apple tree – he was quite right, of course.

After the pleasures of music, the house, garden and many of the people one met there, the other great joy of a stay at Dixter was the food. The generosity of the Lloyd hospitality became legendary, but the quality of it was extraordinary too. Toast and marmalade when made by Christo became ambrosia - despite faithfully following the bread recipe (Daisy's) I never managed to make any remotely as good as his. The Saturday lunch salad was always the platonic ideal of a salad, unequalled before or since. Even if there were just two or three of us for a quiet mid-week supper, the star turn could be turbot or sole fresh from the beach at Hastings, followed by one of his proper steamed puddings – Gentleman's maybe, fragrant with orange and cinnamon, marmalade and breadcrumbs.

If we are lucky we meet one or two people in our lives who change and enrich them profoundly; Christo, for me, was one of those people. He was utterly unique – difficult, endearing, funny, alarmingly clear-thinking – and I count myself as hugely blessed to have enjoyed nearly twenty years of his friendship. For me Dixter and Christo have a golden glow around them, and always will have.

OPPOSITE East Sussex pears stored on racks in the potting shed.

manda: I used to think that Christo disliked children, but in fact he was simply rather wary and unsure of them. The winter after our daughter, Ayşe, was born, Christo, the baby and I spent a lot of time sitting in front of the roaring fire in the great hall together (he could no longer get up to the solar). Christo was fascinated with Ayşe and showed great interest in every sound and movement she made. "Does she need feeding again?" he would ask after every snuffle and cry.

One day, he asked if he could touch her, "as long as it won't hurt her." He cautiously reached out his hand and stroked her arm. There was genuine wonder and delight in his face as she grasped his large fingers tightly and pulled them towards her. He chuckled. I think he felt that she was a little bit his, I hope so.

Amanda Ferguson and Fergus Garrett Amanda Ferguson is married to Fergus Garrett, who worked alongside Christopher Lloyd for fifteen years and is currently head gardener at Great Dixter.

Fergus: Christo became terribly tired in the last few weeks of his life. Hospital life and inactivity didn't suit him – he longed for Dixter, his dogs, and friends.

I visited him every day – he loved and craved company. He often slept, only to be woken by one of us dropping in. When I crept in one day, everything was silent as he lay resting. I held his soft, cold hand in mine and he opened his eyes and squeezed my hand in his. We exchanged no words, just deep feelings.

I'm sorry Christo, that you had to die in hospital. Even though Dixter never left your side, I know you should have been at home.

OPPOSITE The long border on a foggy morning.
BELOW A morning meeting in the parlour between Christopher Lloyd and Fergus Garrett.

My earliest memory of Christopher Lloyd dates back to a visit to Great Dixter in the summer of 1971 when I was sixteen years old and thinking of becoming a gardener. The ancient house, the overflowing garden with its inexplicably uncut grass and Christo selling plants in a temper from a trestle table certainly made an impression.

We met properly in the spring of 1989 when he came to my nursery in Scotland while researching articles en route to Uist. Apart from giving me my first mention in the national press, he wrote me a remarkable letter. When rereading it again today, I can see is full of intuition and good advice. Having apologized for not getting in touch before (this from our greatest, and busiest, gardener) he is encouraging about the nursery before moving on to some character analysis that manages to be both frighteningly accurate and affectionate. I remember wondering at the time why this famous person, who I hardly knew, had gone to all this trouble. I believe it all came down to his need to nurture the people he approved of so that they might get the most out of their lives. As he put it in his letter, "People, after all, are even more important than plants."

My final memory is of saying goodbye at the hospital, with hollow optimism and then returning to Dixter to wait for the phone call. As this came snow began to fall, as if the great event was mirrored in nature. The house and the people in it became quiet – but not for long. Soon the energy and endless reasons to be cheerful that Christo inspired won through and are going strong today. Through his garden, house, books and people, these qualities will persist into the distant future.

Michael Wickenden is the owner of Cally Gardens, a nursery that specializes in unusual perennials.

OPPOSITE *Euphorbia donii* under a light covering of snow.

The richness of any stay at Dixter was curiously enhanced by never really knowing how you were going to be received by Christo from one day to the next, or even one hour to the next. As a generous mentor, you simply couldn't help but seek his favour, but to do so put you in danger of a eliciting a cold dismissal, or of incurring his deeply cutting derision. His wrath was easier to cope with than both the former, thanks to its over-the-top theatricality.

I never saw this better displayed than the night when I locked him out of Dixter. He was out playing bridge when I inadvertently bolted the front door, before heading off to lounge about in the yeoman's hall. By the time I realised what I'd done and let him in, he'd been wandering around outside the building, calling out and knocking on doors for ages. Fury doesn't quite describe his reaction. I stood in the hall, silent and repentant, as he walked back and forth in front of me, screaming fit to burst. I understood his anger and indignation about being locked out of his own home, but when the display grew enormously disproportionate to the sin, I was bold enough to – gently – tell him so. This could have pushed the situation either way, but to his credit, he accepted the point, cooled to about seventy per cent heat output and shuffled off to bed.

He apologized the next day, but in doing so he recounted the events again and made another reference to my thoughtlessness and stupidity, before realizing that he was about to nullify the apology and backed off.

Over a summer staying at Dixter, years of correspondence and a trip to visit my wife and me at our house in Australia, I found that Christo could be like the worst sort of harping, irritable and hyper-critical parent, but simultaneously the most generous, affectionate and affirming friend. He seemed to manage both extremes and everything between in a rich, lovable and highly addictive balance.

Michael McCoy is a garden designer, author, broadcaster, speaker and obsessive home gardener.

Susie Steiner enjoyed a long-running collaboration with Christopher Lloyd during his long tenure as gardening columnist for *The Guardian*.

It is rare in the newspaper world for a columnist to retain their slot beyond a few years. Most tend to lose their freshness or they begin to dash off their columns for an easy fee. This never happened to Christo. Christopher Lloyd was *The Guardian's* gardening expert for seventeen years. He filed his columns right up to his death in January 2006. Some of his best were sent in from his final stay in hospital, bang on time, despite his being in some discomfort.

I admired Christo for so many reasons but chiefly for his ability to lead a truly creative life. He loved gardening and he loved writing and these sustained him into old age. They combated loneliness. Thoughts about his garden, his memories and writing about both got him through the dreary winter when everything looked barren. "When the weather is foul and we are not in the least tempted outside," he wrote, "Or, indeed, when the weather is beautiful but the day ends quite early in the afternoon – these are the most enticing moments for catalogue browsing. To be transported to another world: what bliss!"

I was twenty-nine when I took over *The Guardian's* gardening pages and Christo was in his seventies. At first, we developed a grandfather-granddaughter type relationship. I remember my first visit to Dixter when he walked me round the garden, laughing at my horticultural ignorance. We sat by the fire in his magnificent drawing room and he delighted in giving me a box to open out of which sprang a toy spider, making me jump. He couldn't stop giggling.

He talked about his mother – her gardening prowess and how he managed to wrest his own gardening style from under her shadow. I think pulling out the rose garden and creating his tropical area in its place was a statement of this. He was a gentle iconoclast, loving the clash of brights, taking delight in unusual pairings of plants, championing the dahlia.

Over the years we developed a creative editor-writer partnership. When I had to call him to tell him I thought a column wasn't working (he had a habit of lambasting the visiting public, especially when they messed with his beloved dachshunds), he would huff and puff but he would always rework and refile. My favourite projects with Christo were the series we devised together – one, for example, on essential gardening skills such as digging and watering; another on his memories of the gardening greats who had been part of his life, from Gertrude Jekyll to John Treasure.

I visited Dixter often and even into his eighties he always cooked for us himself, usually a delicious meal of fresh fish with vegetables and herbs from the garden. The house was always full of friends who adored him. He was always grateful to his loyal staff at Dixter who made his creative life possible. And his love for Fergus knew no bounds. Christo loved young people, not in a patronising way but with a real interest. He would cup his ear with a mischievous smile to listen to you. He would laugh a lot and he had a naughty sense of humour.

I think of him when I am gardening now. I have grown to share his dislike of roses but I have a girlish attachment to camellias – "Those smug little rosettes of colour," as he disdainfully put it. But what he approved of most was having your own point of view: "At the least, you must react somehow," he said. "If you accept all your surroundings meekly, something in you will die."

Wayne Winterrowd and
Joe Eck are co-founders of
the garden design firm
North Hill, and live in
Vermont, U.S.A. Their
book *Our Life in Gardens* was
published in 2009.

On our bathroom sideboard there is a picture of Christopher Lloyd that winks at us every morning. It is the one of him looking quite portly in a tweed jacket, with a wise-looking dachshund tucked under his arm. We do not know whether the dachshund is Tulipa, or Dahlia or the most unfortunately named Yucca, who was the last Dixter dachshund. Whichever it is, it looks quite amiable in Christo's loving embrace, but except with him, that was never true of any of his dogs who were – to a one – beasts. Christo wanted his dogs that way, because they were his particular friends and he preferred them to be focused solely on him and feisty towards others.

OPPOSITE *Dahlia* 'Ann Breckenfelder'. ABOVE Canna sleeps while Yucca keeps watch.

And so was he, making as much a speciality of that as his dogs. Many people left Great Dixter bruised and battered, wondering how they had got on the wrong side of him. He could bring blunt speaking to the level of a high art. Once, for example, as we walked expectantly up the front walk, he barked this greeting to us. "You have been away too long and you have got TOO fat!" Not exactly what one would call a warm welcome, though it was, in its candour, bluntness and affection.

When Christo was alive, if you wished to remain welcome in the special world Great Dixter was (and is still), you had to learn quickly to give as good as you got. We once stood with him before a particularly garish planting scheme beside the shed that flanks the old rose garden, made up of a mish-mash of vivid marigolds and other things probably left over from the nursery beds and tumbled all together. "I bet you hate that," Christo said with his dangerous wink. "Actually," one of us replied, "I do." Christo smugly replied "Oh, I was hoping you would say that!" In our own garden he once asked, "Are all these rhododendrons hardy?" When we said they certainly were, he replied, "Pity!"

But beyond his crusty manner – of which he became a great practitioner in his later years (perhaps his earlier ones too, though we did not know him then) – Christo had a deeply generous soul. He cooked lunch and dinner for his guests and he cooked very well. We will never forget the taste of his banana pudding, made to a recipe of his mother's, with maple syrup from America poured on top of it. We'd duplicate it if we could, though we do not wish to do that, because the memory remains special, in its own place.

One particular instance of his generosity remains vivid in our minds. Late one October, we were at Dixter after hard frosts had come. One of us noticed a clump of *Paris polyphylla*, a plant we had been seeking for a long time. We commented enthusiastically on its remains, before continuing our stroll through the garden until Christo left us. We assumed he had gone to prepare dinner, but he returned a while later, extending a dirty hand with three corms in it. "What's that?" "It is what you asked for!"

Paris polyphylla thrives here in our garden in southern Vermont, one of Christo's many gifts to us. Our plants of it are so far from Great Dixter, and yet in a way, so close.

Paris polyphylla.

At least, memory makes it that way. If gardens can be relatives, we think of ourselves as distant cousins. And when we
look at our rhododendrons, thriving so well here, we will
always remember his witty scorn.

"Pity!"

I first knew Christo when I was a garden designer in the seventies. We became friends after having a terrific row on paper and having resolved that, were friends for life. The great thing about him was that he was so incredibly funny as well as being a great gardener. To remember Christo I have turned to his letters, which were so much a part of him:

> It is Thursday morning and I have already been interrupted, by two charming ladies who have been misled by the garden literature to believe what they wanted to believe, namely that we are open in the mornings, not to mention all night as well as the afternoons, and one of them has to return to her home in Cumbria within seconds and this is her only chance.
>
> More tulips; hurrah! But I have to warn you, however, that beautiful as they look in rough grass, they do really need topping up every year. It is not the location of their choice.

And finally: "You have a way of making me feel twice the person I know myself truly to be."

However, anyone who went to Dixter knew Christo actually to be the person he felt his friends made him.

Sonia Coode-Adams and her husband Giles are the co-creators of Feeringbury Manor Gardens, Essex.

Christo, as others have written, was extremely fond of our cousin Pamela Milburn. One winter, our aunt Mavis and her husband, Bill Bayles, were staying with her at Weeks Farm and Christo had been invited for dinner. While Pamela was busy cooking in her tiny kitchen, they were chatting in the dining room beside a roaring fire. Bill got up to stoke the fire and Christo suddenly burst out, "Leave it alone!" as if he owned the house.

Pamela Milburn lived at Weeks Farm, Egerton. Christopher Lloyd was a regular visitor there and often wrote about Weeks Farm in his articles for *Country Life*. Pamela Milburn's cousins Sue and Gill Duff have provided this recollection.

Some years after an infamous scrumping (apple steal-ing) incident that took place at Dixter, Christo came upon Marlon and a friend fishing in the horse pond (pictured below) and was understandably enraged. After ticking them off at length he asked if they'd caught anything but they replied that they'd caught nothing so far. "Well," said Christo, "If you do catch anything, mind you throw it back," and walked off. He seems to have been remarkably tolerant to the village children, although he did later catch Marlon's friend on the back of the head with an apple dur-ing another aborted scrumping mission!

Marlon Dunk is a Northiam neighbour who lives within a stone's throw of Great Dixter. He recounted to Patrick Rice-Oxley his early connection with Dixter as a scrumper and illicit fisherman.

H. B. McKenzie Johnston
is a retired diplomat and
ombudsman.

I was in the same house at Rugby School with Christo. We were not particularly close friends, partly because he had entered the school a year before me and partly because he was intellectually inclined whereas I was more interested in sports, which were not his cup of tea. But we were both learning modern languages and we shared a love of music, as we both played the piano as well as instruments in the school orchestra.

Four of us in our house sometimes performed together in trios or quartets with Christo on the oboe, K. D. Jamieson on the bassoon, me on the flute and R. H. Bennett on the piano. When Christo was invited to be on BBC Radio 4's Desert Island Discs his first choice was the second movement of Poulenc's Trio for Oboe, Bassoon and Piano, which three of us had previously performed in a school competition (although this time with me on the piano). He was very annoyed that in the recorded programme Jamieson's and my names were omitted from the credits. Alas, I am now the only one from this little music group still alive, but the memories of it live on. And I was very fortunate to have been able to renew contact with Christo a few years before he died, and to have been invited, along with my wife, to stay at Great Dixter.

The *Well-Tempered Garden* was my bible as a beginner gardener, so I was very curious to meet Christo in 1992 when mutual friends asked me to set up a long weekend of garden visits in Provence for himself and Fergus. Two days before they arrived, I received a copy of my first book, *Gardens in Provence*. When they arrived, I showed it to my guests, heart in mouth, before Christo took one look at it and said, "Now, why would anybody put a half dead Virginia creeper on the cover of a book!" My husband, rarely at a loss for words, said to him with a grin, "You know, you are a terrible person!" Christo looked really pleased and answered, "Yes, I am!" A highlight of that trip was a visit to La Louve, where we were received by its owner and creator, Nicole de Vésian, then nearly eighty. Three years later, Christo wrote about her in a letter to me: "How could I or anyone else forget her? Such an individualist! That is rare and a treat when met." It seems to me that this comment is just as appropriate for Christo.

Louisa Jones has lived in southern France for over thirty years. Her many books include *Gardens in Provence* and *The Garden Visitor's Companion*.

Rheum palmatum atrosanguineum and *Tulipa* (unknown).

TRAVELS

Christo arrived, bustling in, clutching his ancient overnight bag. The cracked leather peeling like ancient fish scales. From it he extracted a brown paper parcel and offered me sandwiches, his own homemade bread and sweet ham. It was the beginning of a unique adventure. BETH CHATTO

This sequence of photos was taken by Aaron Bertelsen one Easter when Christopher Lloyd and Beth Chatto were on holiday staying at Kerdalo Gardens in Brittany. It shows them looking at a euphorbia in Isabelle Vaughan's garden.

When Vicky and I moved to Dogwood, our present home near Ullapool in northern Scotland, Christo was our very first visitor. The entry in our visitors' book for 11 June 1997 reads: "This will make a very decent staging post." He loved Scotland and came back every autumn to visit friends and their gardens. The following year he wrote: "You are quite right to be over the moon about Dogwood, as I told Beth Chatto last year. Keep it up and find happiness." Two years later, "Me again. I think you're doing very well all things considered. General fossilisation [a reference to my retirement] is an ongoing danger I hear. Keep it up." In 2003, with our guest room unavailable, he wrote: "Not staying just passing; address somewhere doon Sooth [sic]." His final visit came in 2004 and records his frailty: "We totter on..." On the line beneath his entry his nameless companion/chauffeur added, "Without tact."

Tony Schilling was curator of Wakehurst Place from 1967 to 1991. He is a horticultural consultant, lecturer, author, and Honorary President of the Tree Register.

He was the quintessential homebody. It is hard to imagine someone more in love with and in tune with his home ground. But Christo also loved travelling, whether around the corner in East Sussex to visit the old churches on the Romney marshes or halfway around the world to explore the gardens and landscapes of New Zealand, America, Turkey, or South Africa. He had only two conditions: he preferred people's homes to hotels, and he disliked wasting time getting to his destination.

Christo assessed a driver's ability by two measures: a willingness to pass other drivers on the road, no matter what; and an ability to come to an immediate stop whatever your speed in a hundred yards or less. On a trip to South Africa in 1999, as we flew along the roads with our hosts Peter and Barbara Knox-Shaw, Christo would suddenly spot a plant of interest and ask sharply, "What's that?" whereupon Peter would quickly put his foot down on the brake pedal, caus-

Christopher Lloyd botanizing in South Africa.

Thomas C. Cooper,
a former editor of
Horticulture magazine, lives
in Massachusetts, U.S.A.

ing the car to shudder and the four of us to brace against the nearest surface. A brief, satisfied smile would pass over Christo's face as we ground to a halt.

Late one afternoon, on our way home to Peter and Barbara's house outside of Cape Town, Christo glimpsed a brief flutter of white at the brow of a steep banking that rose up from the road. Peter stood on the brakes, and we lurched to a stop. Twenty-five feet above us, just at the crest of the steep hillside, was a small specimen of what Peter thought might be Cape anemones, *Anemone capensis*. Christo raised his eyebrows in an expression both of excitement and childlike challenge. The slope was steep and tangled with shrubs and small trees. It had been a long day already, and Christo admitted it looked like a struggle for him. But he had never seen this plant in the wild, and he liked nothing better than seeing a plant in its native habitat. So we hauled our way up, with Peter giving Christo a hand from the front, Barbara and I pushing from the back, and Christo punctuating the exertions with hoots of laughter at our stumbling progress.

The climb led us to a scrappy patch of open ground studded with the husks of dead proteas that had been burned by the fires that regularly sweep the region. And, yes, there were a couple of patches of the delicate anemones, their milky white petals fluttering in the fading light. Christo quickly got to work with his camera and his notebook – essential items, along with a pocketknife. He noted the site, the conditions and the plant's character. He would expand on these notes later, back in his room. Then the three of us sat down to watch the plants sway against the mountain backdrop. After a few minutes, Christo said, "Well, I think it's almost time for a whisky," and we headed back down to the car.

Most gardeners met Christo through his writing. That's how I did, aged eighteen, when I was living in Alaska and renting a deceased neighbour's home and overgrown garden. I had inherited a small library of books from my neighbour of which one was *The Well-Tempered Garden*. I had heard of the author and knew a little about the mixed border which he was credited with devising at Great Dixter. We Alaskans had always had mixed borders, to ensure that our gardens survived our brutal and unpredictable winters. I wondered if by reading the book I would learn anything new about gardening from Christopher Lloyd.

His writing was pithy, literate, and eye-opening for me. I didn't know that garden writing could be so good (I had yet to read the books by Graham Thomas, Beth Chatto and others in my newly acquired library). He used botanical names that were mostly new and unpronounceable to me, but I was intrigued and read on, mentally mumbling through the Latin bits. Clearly this Lloyd fellow did know something and could teach Alaskans ways to improve our mixed borders. He understood microclimates. He loved and used annuals as much and as wildly as we did.

That spring, I began to dare to mix any kind of plants in my borders and plantings. Alaskans had always mixed parsley and cabbage with flowers, but now I used other vegetables with roses, shrubs, bulbs and trees. Carrots became border edgings. Colour combinations of yellow and pink created new brilliance in the well-lit nights of the midnight sun. It was liberating. This man and his garden seemed fantastic.

Twenty years later, in the early nineties, I first came to the gardens at Great Dixter. Actually I was only able to visit the nursery as the gardens were closed, so I peered over fences and hedges to catch a glimpse of it. It looked like a medieval village with gardeners and house staff moving about everywhere. The nursery was a seeming jumble of plants for sale with others on display but not for sale. I couldn't believe

Jim Fox works as a bulb & rhododendron buyer for Wells Medina Nursery in Washington, U.S.A.

it was a functioning business. The office door was so low I had to bow down to reach it. The door also had an odd sign hanging above it saying, "Duck or Grouse." What on earth did that mean? Surely Lloyd wasn't selling game meat in there too! Though I wouldn't have been surprised if he had been.

On my next visit a year or two later, the house and garden were open. The meadow, full of dying grasses, a few bulbs and some wildflowers oddly placed in front of the house, was curiously appealing. It was not just a bit of unkempt land but was clearly the result of many years of thought and work. It was a garden. The upper gardens, however, made no sense to me. There were jumbles of mixed plantings held in place by hedges. "Sissinghurst did this much better," I thought. How had Lloyd got it so wrong? Nothing here matched what I had read in his writings. Only years later did I learn that this area was essentially a nursery or trial area that served the long border and other parts of the gardens.

Walking down the stairs and paths through this visual cacophony, I could see a meadow and an orchard through an opening in the massive yew hedge. Once I was through this opening, the long border spread its wings on either side of me. It was at that moment that I had my epiphany at Dixter. Here was a brilliant combination of shapes and colours. It was a planting as well crafted as a meticulously planned dinner party, one with each guest highlighting the one next to them. At the far end was the host - the timber house anchoring it all to the land. This was magic. This was joy. This was someone having fun on his own terms. This was what the man had been writing about all along.

On future visits, the border never lost its joie de vivre and originality. Other parts of the garden were more mutable or inscrutable to me, some positively nonsensical to me. But always, as with his writing, I was provoked - to question my own work or even the design in front of me. Why did he do it? What was the reason? Was it play? Was it really thought out? Or was it quickly planted at the end of a tiresome day? I was intrigued and inspired.

It was in Portland, Oregon, U.S.A., that I finally met Christopher Lloyd. I'd met his head gardener, Fergus Garrett, a couple of years earlier and we had become instant friends. It was he who insisted I meet the man and not to be afraid of what I'd heard about him - and I'd heard a lot. Fergus said I would get answers to many of my questions.

Before the lecture, Fergus introduced us, saying "Jim will help you with anything you need if I'm not around, Christo." That was news to me. The man just looked over his glasses at me, said "I'm Christo," and held out his hand in greeting. We sat backstage and ate lunch. He was gruff. I tried to sound confident in what I did know – and be open about what I didn't know. The looks over the glasses became less severe. Christo and I began to find some ease with each other.

While Fergus gave his lecture, Christo and I sat in the audience. After a few minutes I could hear soft sighing and slow breathing next to me. The great man was napping, chin nicely resting on chest. Fergus continued on. At one point he made an unsure comment about some RHS Aquilegia trials. The napping man next to me popped his head up suddenly and said loudly, "It's the blue one, Fergus, which does better, having a fuller form and a better resistance." Just as quickly back went the chin to the chest and the soft breathing resumed. This man missed nothing – even during a nap.

After the talk my job was to move people through the autograph line, to keep any one person from taking up too much time or pressing him for impossible favours. Having worked for a senator before, this wasn't difficult. Christo seemed pleased at the end of our task. "Well, we made it through that group without too much damage. Now I need to go to the bathroom. Can you show me the way?" I offered him my arm as he was a bit wobbly by this time of day and after sitting for so long, but he rejected it and clasped his hands behind his back and said, "Just walk ahead and I'll follow behind." As he later described it to his friends, "As

he was all of six foot tall and over two hundred pounds, Jim just moved ahead while I walked behind him. The crowds parted like the Red Sea before Moses while I followed him, as I kept my head down and went rather unnoticed."

At the bathroom door, he asked me to stand guard, saying, "I've had women walk in here to ask me questions." "You're kidding," I said incredulously. "Not at all. Once one even came in, stood next to me while I was facing the wall, and asked me if I'd autograph one of my books for her. I said, 'Madame, I write with my right hand – and it is currently in use.' So she waited!" After that I stood guard and did actually prevent several female groupies from going in. "Is he in there? Can't I just go in and say hello?" "No," I said. "I think he's occupied." From that day on, Christo referred to me as his bodyguard. I was often mischievously introduced with the line, "This is Jim. He's my bodyguard in America. I'm terribly popular there, you know."

It was in December 2004 that we finally found a mutually free spot in our calendars and I flew to England for a long winter weekend at Dixter. He lived in the great house as easily as he wore his old sweaters, corduroy pants, and worn shoes. He had heard I could cook, so I was to do most of the meals – but no matter what I did, it wasn't right. "No, no, no. You don't cut the ends of the Brussels sprouts! Where did you learn such silliness? Just put them in a pot of boiling water, lid off, for twenty minutes and it boils the wind out of them. That's all they need, along with a bit of butter." And so we spent almost the entire weekend in the kitchen – he cooked while I laid the table and carried the drinks trays.

Some guests came for dinner and others came for lunch. They were as mixed as the plants in the long border – colourful, loud, quiet, dramatic, interesting and well-mixed when side by side, though sometimes there were clashes across the table, egged on by Christo's intellectual mischievousness. He could read a personality quickly and didn't suffer fools at all. "Don't be stupid and speak up about what interests you" might have been his motto.

He loved opera and I began to see his life, his garden and his compositions as one big opera, full of messy and melodious passages and conversational arias, with aged widows passing as youthful ingénues and young men with pretensions worthy of an egomaniac tenor. One quiet passage of our winter weekend opera that I remember most fondly was the clear, cold Sunday morning when I was suffering from jet lag and awoke late. The dining room was empty when I ate my breakfast. I didn't hear the dogs anywhere. No one seemed out in the frosted garden. The logical place to look seemed the solar. Across the big, coldly lit great hall I went, up the wooden stairs to the great clanking wooden door of the solar, where I was greeted by yapping and barking.

"Canna! Yucca! Canna! Be quiet!" Christo yelled out as I opened the creaking door. "Good morning," I said. A massive fire was roaring in the huge old Elizabethan fireplace. "I take it you had a good sleep," he said with an edge of teasing sarcasm. "Yes, very good," I said. "I think it was the jet lag and having a nice cool room to sleep in." He looked at his watch. It was nearing ten o'clock. He took a soft deep breath and I waited for another sardonic rebuke. "You know," he began breathily, "My old friend Sir David Scott used to say, 'One must drink Champagne whilst everyone else is in church.'" He peered at me over his glasses. Where was this leading, I wondered silently. "Do you agree?" asked Christo. "Ah, yes. Why yes. It sounds lovely," I replied. "Oh goody," he said, the look on his face softening like that of a child who's just learned that he's getting a treat before lunch. "Could you go and get it, please? You remember where it is, don't you? And could we have some of the nibblies we had last night with the whisky?"

So that morning, while everyone else was in church, Christo and I polished off a bottle of very good Champagne along with some macadamia nuts and chocolate-covered ginger with Canna under a blanket beside him and Yucca lying so close to the fire I was surprised she didn't burst into

flames herself. We talked about his new book, *Succession Planting*, as the first copies had just arrived. We also spoke about other gardeners, most of whom he thought highly of. I knew he and Graham Thomas didn't get along – like oil and water, as it were. I'd known Graham well, so I was curious to hear Christo's side of the story. What did he think of Graham Thomas, I asked, lulled into brazenness by half the Champagne and the roasting of the fire. In a loud voice with a firm, adamant tone, he replied, "He's a good writer, but he can't brook anyone disagreeing with him. He just wants young people around him to adore him and agree with him and hang on to his every word. He's too opinionated. Things must be his way or he won't listen. Some people find him very likable. Beth does. I don't!" End of discussion. Had I heard right? The Champagne and heat had fogged my brain. I thought I'd asked about Graham Thomas.

The fire crackled on while we remained silent. Christo was tapping slowly on his ancient laptop as one of his weekly articles was due the next morning. At some point he stopped, closed the lid of the computer, put chin to chest and soon we were both dozing off. We both awoke hours later. He opened the laptop, finished the article with a few more taps and announced it was time to make lunch. Served with wine of course. So it went on for the rest of the day and my entire stay at Dixter.

When it was time for me to leave, he was sitting at a table in the great hall doing business with various staff. I interrupted to thank him for his hospitality and say goodbye. "Do come again," he said. "Any time! I quite enjoyed having you here and here's a little memento for you." He handed me a copy of his cookbook. "Suitably inscribed for you," he said with a twinkle in his eye. Then he waved goodbye, his thick fingers dancing and waving in the air, as his staff gathered back around him.

By the time I got my bags, said goodbye to Fergus, and reached the end of the meadow, I turned back to the house for one last look. The sun was shining on the front of the house and the front porch. I was just in time to catch sight of Christo shuffling off towards the upper gardens, the sun lighting up his shock of white hair. He had a tweed jacket on for warmth, a trug under one arm and some secateurs under the other, with Canna and Yucca running at his feet. He was off to see what was looking interesting in the garden and might be good for lunch.

In the car, I opened the book and read his shaky handwriting: "Wish you'd had time to cook for me, Jim. Next time! Great to have you here, especially when we're both saying nothing. Love, Christo." I smiled. He had had fun composing this and knew exactly that I'd be grinning as I read it.

He died just over a year later. At the celebration of his life the great hall was filled with bright new light coming through the diamond-shaped panes of glass in the big windows, across the faces of gathered people ranging between the ages of nine months to over ninety. All his family, friends, and acquaintances were there. There were gardeners from all over the world, house tour guides, housekeepers, woodsmen, field farmers, publishers, authors, photographers, cooks, opera lovers, army mates, neighbours, dinner companions, and plant explorers. Beth Chatto likened Christo to one of the great fires that most of us had sat around with him. "But now Christo's fire has gone out," she said. We were the sparks left to go on and make new fires in new places.

Late that night, as the last of us left Dixter, we walked out into a night where the sky was filled with stars – sparks from so many celestial fires. Orion was standing proudly over the house. I couldn't help thinking of Christo and of all that had been said that day. We paused and wordlessly took it all in. After a while, in the cold quiet, Fergus softly said, "Beth got it right."

Harvesting celeriac.

Laura Gatacre and her
husband, Peter, live and
garden at De Wiersse in the
Netherlands.

Christo shared his birthday with my husband's and on one occasion he and my husband hosted a joint celebration at our house. Romke van de Kaa and Pip were there, along with some of our friends and relations. We invited the Schubert Ensemble because they were all friends of ours and the pianist was our cousin. Christo was a bit put out when he heard that they were to play Fauré's Quartet No. 2 for Piano and Strings for Peter and demanded that he be allowed to choose a piece for himself as well. A little discussion ensued as he first requested Brahms, but in the end William Howard played from Janáček's *On an Overgrown Path* especially for him and he was thrilled.

He was relieved to be able to sleep on the ground floor and not to have to climb two steep flights of stairs. After the celebration, he sent us a letter of which the following lines are extracts:

> The musicians themselves were outstanding and such dear people to meet. The whole gathering was so alive that I couldn't help feeling more alive than usual. . . . I was so comfortable in my room. Thank you for letting me have that one. It may be good for my heart to go up several flights of stairs several times a day, but I was glad not to have to! (A lavatory cleaning brush in the bathroom might be a good idea?) . . . Your *Erythronium dens-canis* is an inferior strain, I'm afraid. Such a shame, but the flowers are pasty and so are the markings on the leaves. When you come in April, we'll dig you up a grand clump of ours (which I originally had from an Irish garden) which you can pull apart in separate units.

This letter is a typical example of Christo's combination of uninhibited criticism and generosity. Both the Dixter *erythroniums* and our own "inferior strain" are still growing in our woodland.

In August 1956 Christo was thinking of writing a book on the influence of Italian Renaissance gardens on English gardens, to be illustrated by his own photographs. He wanted to visit gardens near and in Florence, Sienna, Lucca, Padua and Viterbo. At the botanical garden at Padua (pictured below) he saw six enormous pot jars with small trees in them and wanted a similar jar for Dixter. So we went to Deruta, a famous pottery centre, and found one, which we strapped precariously on the roof of the car and brought it back over the Simplon Pass to England. We were also able to buy at Deruta several bowls, jars and plates ornamented with traditional floral designs to match some similar ones in the kitchen at Dixter.

Roger Highfield met Christopher Lloyd in the army and remained a long-standing friend.

Jeff Jabco is Director of
Grounds and Coordinator
of Horticulture at the Scott
Arboretum, Swarthmore
College, Pennsylvania, U.S.A.

Joe Henderson and I first met Christo when he came to Swarthmore College's Scott Arboretum to speak in 1993. The education coordinator at Scott asked if we would host a speaker coming from England and that this speaker preferred to stay with hosts rather than staying in a motel or guesthouse. We said yes reluctantly, because all that we knew of Christo was that he was an older gentleman from England with a garden that was open to the public, having never been to England at that point. We were concerned that we were going to have a cranky old codger for a guest. When Christo arrived he was perfectly cordial and pleasant. He did let us know that he wanted a nap before dinner and that he preferred whisky (Scotch to us) before dinner. On this first visit Christo stayed for a few days and wowed the audience he spoke to and was a perfectly pleasant visitor when going to the many gardens we visited.

Christo visited and stayed with us several more times over the years, usually by himself, but once with Fergus in tow. On one occasion we arranged for some garden visits. By this time Christo had made quite a name for himself among gardeners in the Philadelphia area. Our close friend, Judy, thought it would be quite a coup if she had Christo come to her garden and stay for lunch. This would give Judy bragging rights for some time! We did arrange for us to visit and stay for lunch. It didn't take Christo long at all to figure out the situation, and he also realized that Judy was working hard to impress him, and that Judy could also take a good amount of serious ribbing. While sitting in the back garden before lunch, Christo looked up at the back of Judy's house and said, "Why do you think your house is so ugly?" Judy was actually speechless, but took the comment very good-naturedly.

During Christo's first visit to stay with us, he asked us what we thought of his garden. When we said that we had never visited it, he said with indignation, "You've been to England, but you never visited Dixter?" We then explained that we had never been to England either. Christo relaxed and said with all sincerity that we should get ourselves to England to visit gardens and that we could stay at Dixter and use it as a base to go out garden visiting. This we later did many times. By staying at Dixter we got to know many British gardening personalities whom we count as friends today.

Christo would always welcome us to Dixter with a small fresh arrangement of flowers from the garden in the bedroom and he would always point out the special view of the garden from the bedroom's windows. Christo always said that in designing a personal garden you should try to make only one person happy – yourself.

When we discussed flowering meadows and Christo's forthcoming book about meadows for days at Dixter, he decided to include the rich natural meadows of Hungary in his work. He wanted to see the different types of Hungarian meadows and take many photos to illustrate the book. I drew up an itinerary and Christo, Fergus and Amanda landed at Budapest airport in early June. First they stayed with us at Vácrátót Botanical Garden. Each morning we started off in a different direction, looking for meadows in bloom. We visited the colourful mountainous grasslands near Lake Balaton, the rolling sandy pasture covered by feather grass between the Danube and Tisza rivers, the alkaline treeless puszta on the Great Hungarian Plane. We waded into the sea of poppy and larkspur on the old waste fields.

Christo commented on everything as usual, the landscapes, the villages and buildings, the gardens and the vegetation. Sometimes he was sarcastic and vitriolic if there was something he didn't approve of. He called on Amanda to take photos of buildings, flower arrangements and plantings, even of things considered ugly by him. We also had many opportunities to taste lots of excellent regional food and

Kósa Géza is the Director of Botanical Gardens at the Hungarian Academy of Sciences in Vácrátót, Hungary.

Common spotted orchids in the meadow at Dixter.

wine at remote village restaurants, and we also tried several sorts of Hungarian fruit spirits, pálinka.

I knew of a very good fish restaurant at a ferry station near the Tisza River and as I knew of Christo's enthusiasm for fish dishes we dropped in for lunch there one day. There was some freshwater fish on the menu and Christo wanted to try a local speciality. We chose harcsapaprikás (catfish with sour cream and paprika) and I also suggested he try the roasted kecsege, which is a speciality in the Tisza River area. Christo had never sampled it before. The waiter remarked that it came as quite a big portion, but Christo said, "It will be fine."

The kecsege was superb, it was sixty centimetres long and lay fragrantly on the plate. Christo looked at it wide-eyed, but he promised he would finish it single-handedly. I was sceptical, but he was true to his word and soon only the backbone was left on the plate. It was really incredible. We drank some wine to the fish and cheerfully went to examine the next flowering meadow.

Christopher Lloyd

f flowers and of the gardens at Great Dixter,
far as he can remember, and he
to take a life-long interest

*Don't I look young? Well,
I was, once. Clive*

and some of his
ws on the rôle of
ciating them with
e holds that plants
n grown together,
ay be achieved in

is present book were
art of this beautifu
tury and the gardens

Marco Polo Stufano was the first Director of Horticulture for Wave Hill, in New York, U.S.A. Marco's involvement led the development of Wave Hill's gardens until his retirement in 2002.

On the first morning of Christo's first visit to my house in New York, he appeared in the kitchen for breakfast and immediately said that he had noticed that I had virtually all his books on a shelf in the guest room. In his playful and twinkling way he asked if I would like to have him sign them. Could there be any doubt what my answer was? I was thrilled and said, "Yes, please!"

Upon his departure, I rushed into the guest room to see what had been written. I was delighted to find that he had written something different in each volume, not just signed them with an expected greeting. His sense of humour and something of the man is revealed in these entries. Among my favourites:

> *The Well-Tempered Garden*: "I rather liked this one. Had to fight the editor."
> *Foliage Plants*: "I could write twice as long a book now. Would it be any better?"
> *The Adventurous Gardener*: "Always extend the frontier."
> *In My Garden*: "How has my writing developed over thirty years?"
>
> And my favourite, referring to his photo on the book's dust jacket (pictured opposite):
> *Clematis*: "Don't I look young? Well, I was, once."

Barbara Paul Robinson is a lawyer, writer and gardener who serves on several boards including those at Wave Hill and Stonecrop Gardens in New York, U.S.A.

Sparkling eyes with a hint of deviltry in them, an engaging smile and there he was. Christo was the honoured guest at Wave Hill, a very special public garden in New York where I serve on the Board. He was also coming to my apartment the next day for a dinner party we had organized for him. When I asked him what he would particularly like on the menu, he replied, "Oysters." "Raw or cooked?" I foolishly asked, not realizing what a gourmet he was. My stupidity was dismissed with his answer "Raw, of course. That's the only way to eat oysters!"

When I simply couldn't quite imagine how to provide a sufficient number of shucked oysters for our party of over twenty people, Christo took his opportunity to tease me mercilessly about it afterwards. His wit could be withering.

He came again some time later to Connecticut where he was part of a programme at White Flower Farm. My country home, Brush Hill, is nearby and he and the distinguished group came for another dinner there. I was smart enough not to ask him what he would like on the menu that time! Given the hilly terrain of part of my garden, I drove Christo around in my golf cart. Always game for some fun, he loved the ride and he was extraordinarily generous in his remarks about my own gardening efforts. Fergus came too and astonished us all with his Herculean ability to throw stones further than we had imagined possible for any mere mortal.

But my happiest Christo memory of all was my last visit to Great Dixter. I went with my husband, Charlie, on a day when the garden was closed to the public. I had visited Great Dixter many times before I knew Christo and had read all his books. I had also visited many of the other famous gardens in England and had lived and worked as a gardener at Barnsley for the late Rosemary Verey. I knew that although Charlie doesn't know plants, his artist's eye would appreciate Great Dixter as a living masterpiece. Christo was the most charming and gracious guide, taking us through the historic house and everywhere in the garden, telling us many stories of its history and his own memories of happy times in the great hall. It is one of the profound joys of my life to have known Christo and to have had this unforgettable day with him at Great Dixter. I am so happy to know that under the inspired leadership of Fergus, Christo's brilliant creation will live on.

Beverley McConnell
and her late husband,
Malcolm, created Ayrlies
Garden near Whitford in New
Zealand.

hristo tumbled into my life when he and Beth Chatto came to stay while lecturing in New Zealand in 1989. I had visited Great Dixter earlier and had also read *The Well-Tempered Garden* avidly, revelling in his turns of phrase, his horticultural knowledge and his economy with words. I knew he was strongly opinionated, but had yet to witness and admire his preferential hearing as a practiced art and safeguard. He was such good company – a delightful guest and so appreciative.

When offered Champagne before dinner (when many New Zealanders drink it), he declared, "Only in the morning," so my husband opened a good bottle for breakfast. Traditions sometimes take root this way. Years later, when Malcolm and I arrived at Great Dixter one morning armed with some Champagne, we happily celebrated the occasion with Christo, his family and Fergus before exploring Dixter, the sharpness of eye dulled but compensated for with an all-pervading ambience.

But there was one exchange that will stay with me forever. I asked Christo if he had to choose between his garden and his writing, which would it be. After a silence, he eyed me directly and said, "I have a love affair with the English language." What a great reply and how fortunate for all of us that he never had to make that choice.

OVERLEAF *Ammi majus.*

EPILOGUE

No-one could ever replace Christo. He was a one off, an incredible character, and knowing him made our lives richer. Each one of us carries our own memories, some shared and some isolated, personal and intimate. He has left his mark in all our lives, thank you Christo for sharing your world. It must also be said that Great Dixter didn't run and flourish with Christo alone, and there was and is a dedicated and loyal team that pour passion into this magical place led by the man. If Dixter is to remain that spiritual and influential place in the future, it is they who should also be thanked.

FERGUS GARRETT

Books by Christopher Lloyd

The Mixed Border, London: Collingridge, 1957; Shrubs and Trees for Small Gardens, London: Pan Books, 1965; Hardy Perennials, London: Studio Vista, 1967; Gardening on Chalk and Lime, London: Pan Books, 1969; The Well-Tempered Garden, London: Collins, 1970; Foliage Plants, London: Collins, 1973; Clematis, London: Collins, 1977; The Adventurous Gardener, London: Allen Lane, 1983; Glyndebourne: The Gardens, with Anne Scott-James, Wendover: The Peterhouse Press, 1983; The Well-Chosen Garden, London: Elm Tree, 1984; The Year at Great Dixter, Harmondsworth: Viking, 1987; The Cottage Garden, with Richard Bird, London: Dorling Kindersley, 1990; Garden Flowers from Seed, with Graham Rice, London: Viking, 1991; In My Garden, London: Bloomsbury, 1993; Planting Your Garden, with Ursula Buchan and Fay Sharman, London: Cassell, 1993; Other People's Gardens, London: Viking, 1995; Gardener Cook, London: Frances Lincoln, 1997; Dear Friend & Gardener: Letters on Life and Gardening, with Beth Chatto, London: Frances Lincoln, 1998; Christopher Lloyd's Gardening Year, London: Frances Lincoln, 1999; Christopher Lloyd's Garden Flowers: Perennials, Bulbs, Grasses, Ferns, London: Cassell, 2000; Colour for Adventurous Gardeners, London: BBC Books, 2001; Meadows, London: Cassell, 2004; Succession Planting for Adventurous Gardeners, London: BBC Books, 2005; Exotic Planting for Adventurous Gardeners, London: BBC Books, 2007; Cuttings: A Year in the Garden With Christopher Lloyd, London: Chatto & Windus, 2007.

Photo Acknowledgements

Aaron Bertelsen 106, 114, 182-3. Giny Best 102-3. Jonathan Buckley 12 top, 13 btm, 14-15, 16, 17, 18-19 btm, 19 btm right, 24, 25 top, 25 btm, 27, 28-29, 34, 36 top, 36 btm right, 39, 47 top, 48, 50, 52-3, 64, 66, 89, 125, 134, 137, 139 top, 139 btm, 160, 161, 165, 174-5, 177, 180, 192. Carol Casselden 20, 21 btm, 30, 32, 35, 36 btm left, 37, 47 btm, 55, 56, 58-9, 60, 61, 62, 72-3, 76-7, 82-3, 110 top, 110 middle, 127, 130-1, 132-3, 135, 149, 151, 152, 169, 172, 202-3. Thomas C. Cooper 184-5. Gerry Dawson 22. Fergus Garrett 80-1, 87, 100-1, 116, 119 top, 120, 166, 188-9, 190-1. Great Dixter Archive by kind permission of the Trustees of the Great Dixter Charitable Trust 96, 97 top. Jerry Harpur 158. Roger Highfield 194. Dan Hinkley 83 btm, 84, 85. Kyle Landt 141. Andrew Lawson 2, 6, 119 btm. Jonathan Lloyd 42, 43. Christopher Middleton 97 btm, 157, 163, 167. Michael McCoy 94. Anna Mumford 113 top. James Nunn 8 (map), 21 top, 40, 41, 47 middle, 49, 110 btm, 113 middle and btm, 154, 179 right. Allan Pollok-Morris 12 btm, 13 top right, 44, 45, 128, 139 middle, 144-5, 178, 204. Barbara Paul Robinson 200-1. Marco Polo Stufano 198 inset. Ken Rawson 107, 129, 146, 147. Joe Rodruigez 198 full page. Perry Rodriguez 156. Stephen Rose 92-3 (painting). David Sellman 90. Sarah Seymour 18-19 top, 25 middle, 26, 31, 65, 67, 99, 108-9, 122-3, 173, 197. Howard Sooley 118, 162, 201 right.